Surviving Steffi

BY EVELYN RAUCH

Although the author and publisher have made every effort to ensure the information in this book was correct at press time, the author and publisher do not assume and hereby disclaim any liability to any party for any loss, damage, or disruption caused by errors or omissions, whether such errors or omissions result from negligence, accident, or any other cause. All quoted dialogue is written as remembered by the author and may not be quoted word for word.

ISBN: 1494729474
ISBN 13: 9781494729479

Dedicated to the second generation whose lives have been forever changed by their parents' struggle to survive.

Acknowledgments

I wish to thank my family, for whom I wrote this book. Their patience, love, and ongoing support spurred me on. My children, Eden and Jeffrey, are my reason for telling this story.

To my friend, Anne Meegan, who held me up during my most difficult moments. Words cannot express my deepest gratitude.

To Gail Bogner, who as a fellow second-generation survivor has walked in my shoes. Your untiring love, friendship, and understanding brought this story to life for me.

To Suzy Shechtman, who listened patiently as I read pages and pages of this book to her. I could not have completed this project without your love and expertise.

To Jackie Faigenbaum, who accompanied me on my journey of discovery, my sincere gratitude.

To Eva Neisser, without your simple expression of kindness, your insight and help, I would have never known my grandmother and mother as I do now.

To Lynda Bogel and my fellow scribblers of the Summer Nonfiction Writing Class at Cornell, without you there would never have been a book. *Bird by Bird* is what opened my eyes to the possibilities.

Last, but not least, to my husband, David. Your support and love is, has, and will always be my lifeline.

Table of Contents

Mother

Mother, home of my soul,
My heart longs for you.
I wandered near and far,
But never found the peace of home.
Oh, no one of all the strange people
Gave me the peace of home.
Everyone only wants to know his own children,
But he does not want to know others.
I have not found anyone
Who understands me as you do.
Who loves me with all the faults
He finds in me.
When I erred and made mistakes
I was heartlessly ignored.
And I felt that only a mother
Could be understanding.
Often during dark nights
I cried, not understanding.
I did not want to continue this life.
I longed for my mother, my mother always
And felt that my mother
Was the home of my soul.

CHAPTER 1

I'll Take Care of Everything

The clock says 3:00 p.m. Mom is nervous about missing the bus. Mom and I are in the car at the bus station having our usual banter. We have been through this a thousand times before. Mom is depressed and doesn't want to go to David's birthday celebration. "You will be better off without me," she says. "You would be better off if I was dead. I want to die." She continues, "I wish you would let me go. How much more can I take? It is you, Evie, who has kept me alive for all these years, and for what?"

"This is too much," I answer. "I can't handle this abuse anymore." I am exploding into a million pieces. "So do it already. I can't listen to it anymore. Thirty years of this is enough. You have to stop badgering me."

Mom kisses me good-bye and says, "You don't need me anymore. Let me go." Before I can say I'm sorry, she opens the door and in an instant she is out on the pavement walking to the bus. I yell after her, but she does not hear me. She looks alone again; so totally and utterly alone.

I am shaking and can hardly drive. The clock says it is now 3:15 p.m. These past fifteen minutes have been agonizing. Why does it always have to end this way? Why in all this time as the clock ticks on and the years go by haven't I been able to make my mother happy? I remember my friend, Gail, saying so wisely, "Our parents have been

1

through too much. They can never be happy. We can only make them proud."

But what could she be proud of today after this terrible altercation? I need to speak to my mother to say, I'm sorry, I didn't mean what I said. But was I really sure that in my deepest of thoughts I really hadn't meant what I had blurted out? This is my mother. She had become a shell of her former self; hollow inside, cynical, and sad. I need to insulate myself. I have become hardened to her pain.

The next day we speak to each other, as we always do, once a day like clockwork. Nothing further is said. The clock ticks on and several days go by. I know my mother is leaving for Southern California on Tuesday to escape the harsh winter. I feel some relief in knowing that she will be with friends in a sunny climate, and that maybe her spirits will be lifted. I will not have to face her and my demons for six more weeks.

It is Sunday. Company is coming. The phone rings. I am rushed. It's Mom. "Evie?"

I interrupt. "Can I call you back?" The faint voice on the line says all right and trails off.

My friends, Susan and Howard, come for brunch. The day is filled with laughter, friendship, and joy. The clock ticks on. It is late. I go to sleep. Monday morning I realize I never called my mother back. I dial. No answer. The clock says 10:00 a.m. I am puzzled that Mom is not home. Maybe she had a last minute beauty parlor appointment?

It is eleven o'clock now and the phone rings. I pick up the phone. It must be Mom. A strange voice on the line says, "Are you Steffi Mannheimer's daughter?" My heart begins to race. I know what is coming. "You better come to your mother's apartment quickly," she says. "I think your mother is in deep trouble. There are notes."

I can't even think; I am paralyzed with fear. This is the phone call that in my heart of hearts I knew someday would come; that terrible moment in time when your whole life changes. If I could only turn back the hands of that clock, maybe things would be different. Maybe I could save my mother from herself.

I glance at my watch. Time is of the essence now. I must get to my mother's apartment; but this could take hours. I call my husband at his office. His secretary tells me he is on a long case in the hospital operating room and will not be back for hours. I am in a state of utter panic. I try to compose myself. I call the hospital and I ask the operator to put me through to the OR. The nurse answers the phone. I tell her that I must speak to my husband. I imagine she can tell by the shaky tone of my voice that I need to speak to him immediately.

She holds the phone to his ear. "David, I think my mother has done something terrible to herself." I begin to cry uncontrollably.

He tells me that I can't go to Mom's apartment alone. He apologizes that he can't go with me and he will get in touch with my daughter, Eden.

"No, please don't call her," I beg "I don't know what I will find."

It is too late. He has already hung up.

It is now 11:30 a.m. Eden is on her way I imagine. I am pacing the floor. The clock keeps ticking. The minutes are going so slowly now. How can I involve my daughter in this? What kind of mother am I? I have tried all of my daughter's life to protect her and shield her from my pain. Now at this crucial moment, I can't protect her at all. I have become the one who needs protection. I am the helpless child.

I sit down alone at the kitchen table. There is an absence of sound. The only voice I hear is my own. How could this be happening? Suddenly the ring of the doorbell breaks the silence. I get up to answer the door. It is my daughter. There are no words said; just a loving kiss on my tearstained cheek.

The clock in the car says 12:30 p.m. It will take an hour and a half to get to Riverdale, New York, my mother's home. The ride through the New Jersey highways, over the George Washington Bridge, and onto the busy traffic-filled streets of New York City seems endless. There are few words said.

It is 2:00 p.m. The elevator is not working. Eden and I climb the steep stairway of my mother's prewar apartment building to the third floor. I am trembling. I pause for just a moment for another kiss on the cheek.

I ring the bell. No one answers. I ring again. No answer. I take my fist and start pounding on the door. Still no one comes. My daughter tries to get me to stop, but I keep pounding on that door. Finally the handyman, who must have been alerted by a nosy neighbor, comes to our rescue.

"Do you have the key to Steffi Mannheimer's apartment?" I ask. "I'm her daughter. I need to get in."

"The police, paramedics, and the ambulance have been here already. They don't want anything touched, but I'll let you in. Her cleaning lady found her this morning when she arrived to clean the apartment. She is the one who called you and found me; then we called the police. I'll leave you both alone now," he says.

"Do you know which hospital they took her to?" I ask.

"Sorry, no, I don't," he answers.

My watch says 2:30 p.m. We enter the apartment. It is dark. There is a stench of vomit and alcohol. I walk ahead of Eden as if I, in some way, could still protect her from what is to come. My poor daughter, twenty-two-years old; this will scar her for life! I take slow, deliberate steps. The bedroom is down the hall and the bathroom across from it. As I continue to walk in front of my daughter, approaching my mother's bedroom, I peer to my right for a moment to look at the bathroom. One split second, one snapshot in my mind. I can't believe my eyes. I quickly close the door of the bathroom before Eden reaches my vantage point. This I can protect her from. We enter the bedroom. On the dresser are several empty bottles of prescription drugs. The bed is unmade and several drawers are open. My mother's half-packed suitcase sits on the other bed in the room. On the bed are several pads of paper and a handwritten note. The writing is hardly legible—several pens have been used in the process of writing it. As I am about to pick up the note, a police officer walks into the room.

"Don't touch anything," he shouts. "Who are you both?"

"I am Steffi Mannheimer's daughter and this is her granddaughter. Please, can you tell me where they have taken my mother?"

The police officer softens his tone. "Your mother is still alive," he says. "They took her to Kingsbridge Hospital."

I feel a slight sense of optimism. Maybe, just maybe, this could all still turn out all right. I ask Eden to call the hospital and find out where she is and how to get there.

I wander across the hall to the bathroom and slowly open the door. The clock inside my head is ticking loudly now as I enter. I am not prepared for what is inside. Taped on the walls are several ripped pieces of paper. They are notes written with an unsteady hand, with specific instructions not to resuscitate my mother. But the one that is most jarring to me is taped to the mirror. It simply says, "Call my daughter. She will take care of everything."

My daughter is calling me from the bedroom. I quickly leave the bathroom and close the door.

"I reached the hospital. Grandma is in the emergency room. They said to bring the bottles of pills."

"We better get out of here and get to the hospital," I cry.

I look at my watch. It is 3:30 p.m. Four and a half hours have passed since the stranger's phone call. There is no time to take anything with us. Just the three empty prescription bottles.

We are descending the steep steps. Running to the car. Time is of the essence. We weave our way through the streets of upper Manhattan, passing the old neighborhood I grew up in. Past the soda shop where I had my first ice cream soda. Past Mother's Bake Shop where all our special occasion cakes came from for birthdays, graduations, Father's, and Mother's Day. We pass the dry cleaners and the supermarket and the Jewish deli where so often when I was growing up we had gotten Sunday night takeout dinner: corn beef, pastrami, coleslaw, pickles, and knishes. Down the steep hill to 231st Street and Broadway under the L where I traveled the subway to Music and Art High School.

Now, somehow, as if by divine guidance, we find our way to Kingsbridge Hospital; a small satellite hospital of Columbia Presbyterian.

We arrive at the emergency room. My mother has been given a drug to revive her and reverse the effects of all the pills. I will never forget the look of anguish on her face as she sees me and Eden enter the room. At this terrible moment I know I have lost my mother forever. There will be no turning back from this. I hold her hand as she lies helplessly in the bed trying desperately not to look into my eyes.

I whisper to her, "It's okay. I know what you want. You don't have to worry. I'll take care of everything."

CHAPTER 2

The Hospital

The clock on the wall in the emergency room says 5:30 p.m. The doctors are trying furiously to stabilize my mother. I plead with them to let her be; not to do anything heroic to save her. Her wish is to die peacefully. They are not receptive to my pleas.

These young doctors have been trained to save lives, not to stand by and watch someone die. My daughter is beside herself. How she, a medical student, must feel at this moment as she listens to her mother begging for her grandmother to be left alone to die. I can feel the tension in her body as she stands by my side. I can feel the adrenaline rising in my own veins. My heart is racing now. I feel each beat scoring each second that goes by.

I have to stay focused. I can't concentrate on my daughter now. My only goal is to allow my mother to die with some dignity, if that is at all possible. I try to calm my nerves. I have to be strong for all of us.

Ever since that horrific day in November 1979 when my mother woke up from unsuccessful brain surgery—a botched operation—I have been fighting to save her life. We have gone through numerous surgeries and hard recoveries just to get poor Steffi fit to live on.

As the hours turned into days and the days into months and the months into years, I have been giving her strength, holding her hand, and making her fight back. All the while her past had left her bitter and angry. Most of that anger was directed at me.

Now she is counting on me to grant her a final wish. I feel the bile come up into my throat. I am standing in the satellite hospital of the same medical center where my mother's brain surgery had been performed so many years before. We had come full circle. Was this to be her final destination?

Each minute seems like an eternity as I wait for the chief doctor in the emergency room to tell me what will happen next. Finally, a doctor approaches me. "Are you Steffi Mannheimer's daughter?" he asks.

"I am her daughter. Can you please tell me what is going to happen to my mother now?"

"We would like to put her on a respirator to help her breathe," he says.

I tell him that she has a living will, and again I emphasize that it would not be her wish to have anything done to save her life.

"Unfortunately," he continues, "in suicide cases the living will becomes null and void because the patient is considered unstable. Therefore, it is up to the doctor of record to determine the course of care for the patient."

"Please, I beg of you, don't put her on a respirator. My mother has suffered enough. She has had years of poor health and has not done this because of one moment of insanity. She has been planning this for years. She is seventy-eight-years-old and her future will be a living nightmare from here on in."

"I understand your feelings and I will try to avoid the respirator," he answers.

I hear compassion in this doctor's voice. Maybe I have an ally now?

The nurse changes the bag on my mother's IV and I am told they will take her up to a room soon. My mother is unconscious again. I am holding her hand. Again there are no words just feelings, so many feelings. I am trying so hard to suppress them all.

The emergency room is filled with people. There is a lot of noise, but I hear nothing. There is utter silence for me. Nothing but the hands of the clock on the wall moving ever so slowly; each tick growing louder in my brain. I feel as if I am in slow motion, in a vacuum. I can only feel Mommy's icy hand in mine. I am frozen in my own fear. How am I going to handle all of this?

My husband arrives. I am filled with emotion that comes pouring out. I can't control it any longer. I am sobbing. "Why is this happening? I am to blame. I should have called her back. She would not have done this if I had called her back! I don't think I can get through this. Please tell me what to do."

"Take one step at a time," he says. "We will see where this is going. Please explain to me what happened."

David's calm demeanor is infuriating. Can't he see how desperate this situation is? How utterly beside myself I am? Can't he understand my daughter is in such pain? We need comfort, not cold logic. I am feeling sick to my stomach again. I am totally out of control. I need to be hugged.

Suddenly a voice in my head says, "You are the mother now. It is your time to be strong. You have to make the decisions and be as unemotional as possible; no one can do this for you."

I feel a hot rush come over me. I have to do this right. I have to think clearly. I realize that I am lucky to have a partner to help me. I have a family—we are not perfect but we love and have compassion for each other. I am not alone in this. Time will tell what we will face next. Time will take its course and we will bear witness.

My mother's nurse interrupts my thoughts and she lets us know that they are moving my mother to a room. She is unconscious and has no knowledge that she is being moved, but I feel her anguish. There is no warmth in her hand, which I hold as we move through the halls.

In contrast to the world outside, everything inside is white, devoid of color and feeling; cold as the icy January sky. There are no pictures on the walls. It feels lifeless and yet the whiteness looks clean and light. I realize this is the psychiatric floor. We enter the room. The walls are also whitewashed as if to camouflage the sadness of the many stories that must have unfolded in this room. There are no embellishments whatsoever on the walls except for a clock at the foot of my mother's bed.

Across from the doorway are four large picture windows that span the wall. Finally there is a glimpse of the world outside. It is beginning to snow. The ground is sprinkled with white snowflakes. There are train tracks. It dawns on me that this must be my mother's waiting station to heaven.

It is now 11:00 p.m. Eden and I have been together, living this nightmare, for twelve hours; an eternity.

The night nurse comes into the room. She assures me that my mother will just rest and that we should go home. Eden has been my lifeline. I never could have gotten through this day without her. I am so thankful to this sensitive, level-headed young woman who I am so proud to say is my daughter. She has always made me proud, but today I can't find the words to describe how much she means to me. How special she is. I can't protect her from this horrific event, but I need to watch out for her as her mother. So I beg my husband and Eden to go home, and ask that only David return in the morning.

"Eden, you have to go home and continue your studies. That is what Grandma would want. She would not want you to see her like this. This was not her intent," I say. There is no argument. With a kiss on my cheek and tears in her eyes, she turns toward her grandmother, kisses her forehead and whispers, "Good-bye. I love you, Grandma."

My mother is sleeping peacefully. Eden and David are gone. I am alone with my mother. The room is warm but my hands are ice. I have to face the fact that my mother is a suicide patient and that is a crime in the state of New York.

CHAPTER 3

The Final Destination

All of this feels surreal. I am living a nightmare. If I just shut my eyes and go to sleep, I will wake up in the morning and this will all be a bad dream.

"Mom, here I am. You have me now—my undivided attention. What you always wanted. Please wake up and want to still be my mommy and live. There is still time to change your mind. I can help. Please don't let go, not just yet. You know my big birthday is coming up and Jeff's graduation from college: How could you want to miss that? There is so much to live for. There is so much yet to be part of. How could you want to leave me? How could I mean so little to you? How could you be so angry to punish me like this?"

My thoughts are racing around in my head. I don't know which emotion is the strongest. The anger, the sadness, the panic, or the deep love I feel for the mother I never truly understood.

There is deafening silence. My mother's limp body is turned away from the window. She has shut out the world outside. She is already on her way to another world. She looks peaceful, as if she is sleeping. I dim the lights. The snow continues to fall, and I can see in the moonlight that it is coming down heavier now. The decisions that I will have to make in the days to come are weighing heavily on me. For now I just close my eyes. Maybe my mind will take a rest. Maybe sleep will quiet my unquiet mind.

I remember that on the nightstand next to my mother's bed there was a copy of the book, *An Unquiet Mind*. I wonder how many nights she stayed awake unable to control her emotions, and whether she had gained comfort from that book. I wish I had it now to read.

I am awakened by the creak of the door to my mother's room. The light is back on, and I slowly begin to focus on a tall, beautiful young woman entering the room. She, too, is wearing white.

"Hello," she says, and introduces herself. "I am the resident on call this evening. I will be taking care of your mother. Do you think you can answer some questions? I understand that you are refusing the respirator."

I look at this lovely young doctor, and a smile comes over me. She reminds me of my daughter, and my sense of loneliness begins to fade.

"Yes, of course. I don't know what I can offer, but I will be happy to try to answer anything I can," I tell her.

She begins by asking me if my mother had any preexisting medical conditions that she should be aware of, if I know what drugs she took, if she was a substance abuser, and if she had made any other attempts on her life.

I am thinking that so many times during these eighteen years and even long before her poor health issues, my mother has threatened to kill herself. It has become her mantra, and we have become immune to it. No one, after all this time, has ever thought she would actually do it. But she lived alone, and the loneliness had taken its toll. She must have been hoarding sleeping pills for years and I had no idea.

I wasn't sure about alcohol abuse, but there have been times when she seemed to be unsteady. I had always attributed that imbalance to the brain tumor, but maybe it was due to a couple of drinks. Maybe that was why she was so mean at times. I wasn't sure of anything anymore.

I am not sure how much information I should actually share with this young doctor. I want to plead my mother's case and not make her out to be mentally unstable.

I try to quiet my emotions before I speak. I need to sound in control and honest. I begin by saying, "My mother, Steffi Mannheimer, has endured a lifetime of pain and suffering. Our family has suffered along with her. Her medical history would fill a medical textbook. She has endured unsuccessful brain surgery to remove an acoustic neuroma, which caused a straight (nerve damage to her brain stem), paralyzing the right side of her face and upper body. Many operations were performed just to make her fit enough for life. She can not close her right eye and has had several surgeries to correct this as much as possible so that she would not cause a corneal abrasion. Still she has to wear a hard patch taped to her face at night to protect her eye. My mom was left without a gag reflex on her right side. She chokes frequently on her food and aspirates. This has caused numerous cases of pneumonia. Because the right side of her mouth does not move, the food she eats does not stay in her mouth very well and she drools. She has had several plastic surgeries to help this, but the right corner of her mouth is still paralyzed. Her vocal cords are partially paralyzed so it is hard sometimes for her to speak. The neuralgia she feels never goes away. She has painful inoperable spinal disease, which in the last years has become unbearable. We have consulted with several doctors who have tried numerous treatments to give her some relief, but she is still in constant pain. She has had emergency gallbladder surgery due to a burst gallbladder and infection. We have tried everything; every treatment we could find just to make her fit to live on, and yet she never wanted to be kept alive. She has been a prisoner in her own personal hell. Ever since the day she woke up in this same hospital from the operation to remove her acoustic neuroma, she has wanted to die. You must understand, my mother was in the fashion industry before all this happened to her. Can you imagine how devastating these eighteen years have been for her?"

I suspect when this lovely woman walked into my mother's room she had no idea what she was walking into. I am about to tell the doctor that my mother would not want anything done to save her, when her beeper goes off and she excuses herself to take a call at the desk. I am relieved that she has left the room because I can feel the tears I have been fighting back begin to stream down my face. I am sitting alone again facing the clock, which now says 1:30 a.m. It is a new day and the psychodrama has begun.

Minutes pass. I can't sit alone any longer. I leave the room for the first time and walk down the hall to the desk. The young resident is just getting off the phone. She turns to see me, and in a very sympathetic voice says, "That was the chief attending doctor on the phone. He asked me to fill him in on what I know about your mother's case. He will be coming by to speak to you and examine your mother. I am terribly sorry for all you and your family must be going through, but I have to get all the details so we can determine Steffi's treatment plan."

A feeling of panic comes over me. What are they planning to do to my mother? I have to explain again that it would not be her wish to have anything done to save her life. This doctor will not understand. I know from my daughter's medical school training that these young doctors are trained to value every life, and to do everything in their power to save their patients. How do I tell this young doctor that I want her to leave my mother alone and let her die? She will never consent to that.

"I can see that you are a compassionate person. I understand that you are looking out for my mother's best interests, and I feel I can speak freely on my mother's behalf." I look straight into her eyes and, as convincingly as I can, I say, "My mother truly has reached the end of her life. I have tried for many years to make my mother see that she has much to live for, but in the end it has been for naught. She has nothing left to fight with and any intervention will only prolong her agony. Please understand, I love my mother, but I can't see her suffer anymore."

The young doctor looks distraught. She doesn't know what to say to me. She pauses for a long, deep breath and then says, "The chief attending doctor on call will be here soon. He will speak to you. Meanwhile, we will keep your mother as comfortable as possible. I am so sorry."

With that I turn back down the hall and walk slowly to my mother's room. At least nothing will be decided until the chief attending arrives. In her room the moonlight outlines my mother's frail body. She is still unconscious. I sit back down in the chair and glance up at the clock. Another hour has passed. A veil of sleep comes over me, and I give in to it.

I am awakened once again by the night nurse who has come to check my mother's vital signs. The clock reads 4:30 a.m. and I wonder how long it will be till I meet the chief attending doctor.

CHAPTER 4

The Last Days

The sun is beginning to rise. It has stopped snowing. Outside of the large picture windows the icy snow glistens in the morning sunrise. The world outside is waking up to a new day. But within these white-washed walls nothing has changed.

It is 6:30 a.m. and the doctors are beginning to come onto the floor to make their rounds. I wonder when I will meet the chief attending doctor. I shudder in anticipation of what I must confront next. I feel drugged from lack of sleep, and I hope I will have my wits about me to face what I know is going to be a very difficult day. I hope David will arrive soon so that I will not be alone.

At 7:35 a.m. a handsome man in his early forties, I imagine, wearing a white coat enters the room. He introduces himself as the doctor who will be responsible for my mother's care from now on. He says, looking down at the chart, "I would like to examine Mrs. Mannheimer. Would you please step out of the room for a moment?"

I feel strange leaving my mom alone even for a moment, as if I have been sent to be her guardian and her protector. But I am afraid to question him. I need his cooperation. So without a word I walk out into the hall. After just a brief time, I am invited back into the room.

"I understand that you are refusing any treatment that would save your mother's life. Could you please tell me why?" he asks.

I begin by telling him that everyone has been so kind since we arrived at the hospital. Then I repeat everything I told the resident the night before, putting special emphasis on my mother's wishes not to be resuscitated. The doctor holds my hand, walks me back out into the hall and says, "Don't worry. We will do our best to keep your mother comfortable. We will hang an IV for nourishment then we will leave her alone and just watch her. I will check on her later."

I feel somewhat relieved that he seems to be respecting my mother's wishes and I return to the room. David has just arrived. He hugs me tight. We say nothing. What is there to say? He has brought me breakfast. I have no appetite, but the coffee warms my body and relieves the chill in my veins. I let him know about the visit from the attending physician, and that for now they will just maintain her fluid level and hold off on any further treatment.

"David, I don't know where this is going and I am very scared," I say.

He repeats what he said last night. "Just take this one step at a time."

We sit staring at my mother's motionless body for what seems like a lifetime. Several nurses come in at different intervals to take Steffi's vital signs. We sit in silence; there are no words. The clock ticks on.

It is 12:30 p.m. when the attending physician arrives. I introduce him to David. He seems less friendly than he was this morning.

"I have spoken with the ethics committee of this hospital," he says. "They feel that your mother should be on life support given the circumstances. Suicides are a crime in the state of New York. So she no longer has a say in her destiny. My hands are tied, but if you wish you can speak on your mother's behalf. If you come to the desk I will try to get the chairman of the ethics committee on the phone. Also, there will have to be a nurse in the room with you at all times from now on. This is a legal issue. I am sorry."

I feel the blood drain from my body. How will I ever be able to convince an anonymous person on the phone, who has never met or even seen my mother that keeping her alive would be a crime in itself? How could a committee make such a decision without so much as a visit to my mother's bedside? I need some time to collect my thoughts. To figure out what words will convince them to change their minds. I realize the irony in all of this. For eighteen years I have fought to keep my mother alive. So many times I have confronted doctors, pleading for them to help her, to find a way to make her comfortable so she would be able to live on. Now on this frigid day in January, I was going to fight my biggest battle to let her die. I really don't know if I am up to this last encounter. But my mother put me in charge. "Call my daughter. She will take care of everything." So I ask the doctor if I can just have a few minutes to think before he makes the call.

"I will meet you at the desk," he says. "Take your time. I will wait for you."

A lifetime could not prepare me for this moment, never mind a few minutes to compose myself. What will I say? I want my mother to want to live. How can I fight to end her life? David hugs me so hard I can hardly breathe, and with a tender kiss says, "You can do this. You speak so well. You can convince them. They will listen to you."

With that encouragement, I walk slowly alone, hands trembling, to the desk.

"I'm ready now."

The doctor dials an in-house number, says a few introductory words, and then hands me the phone. The voice on the other line asks me if I am Steffi Mannheimer's daughter, and I answer in the affirmative. He tells me that it is the hospital's policy to put all suicide patients on life support if the attending physician feels the patient requires it. In Steffi's case, he feels she does.

The chairman asks me, "Don't you want your mother to live? She may have just been depressed, and in a moment of weakness taken this drastic step."

He asks if I knew that my mother was seeing a psychiatrist, because he prescribed her sleeping pills. I actually did not know this. She kept it from me. So often I begged her to see someone. But I do not let him know that. I calmly tell him as I told the other doctors before, that my mother had not done this to herself in a moment of despair. That she had suffered for much of her lifetime, and that by her own hand she wished to put an end to her suffering. I beg him to understand the depth of her pain, how I loved my mother, and how I knew that keeping her alive would be cruel and unusual punishment. At her best, she decided to end her life. I ask him to please let her die in peace.

There is silence for a long time. Then the voice on the other end of the phone, a man I never met who is now deciding my mother's fate, says, "You have thirty-six hours, and then we put her on life support."

CHAPTER 5

Thirty-Six Hours

I put the receiver down slowly and stare straight into the attending doctor's eyes. "Thank you," I whisper. "We have thirty-six hours before you have to intervene."

Maybe in these thirty-six hours my mother can still control her own fate. I have done what I can for now. Time and God will have to decide how this will play out. This is a bizarre race against time. No matter the outcome, there will be no happy ending to this horror story.

I return to my mother's room. David is sitting next to my mother's bedside. He tells me to come quickly, that my mother is conscious. I can't believe this is happening. No one is in the room with us. I ask my mom if she would like some water and she nods yes. She slowly sips a few drops through a straw. I then ask her if she wants us to help her, to get the doctors to save her, and she shakes her head violently no.

Before I can say anything else, she is unconscious again. What should I do now? Do I respect my mother's wishes or save her at all costs? How can I make these decisions? Only God should make these decisions.

My back is to the door. I am staring at my mother's unconscious body. I am about to scream hysterically when David, who is facing the door and me, puts his hand to his lips to silence me. As I turn around I am face-to-face with the attending doctor and a stranger, a stout lady in her late fifties.

"Mrs. Rauch, this is the nurse I told you about. She will be with you and your mother at all times from now on."

"Hello," the nurse says. "I am so sorry about all this, but as you know by law you must have someone with you at all times. I know this is a private matter, but there is no alternative so I will try to stay out of your way."

I now have a watchdog who will report everything that goes on in this room. I can't speak freely. I am being scrutinized at all times from here on in. The only place that is safe is the end of the hall. There is a large picture window with a sill that I can sit on. David and I will have to go there to speak freely to each other.

This outsider has added a new strain to an already unbearable situation. Her reluctant presence has created an uneasy tension in the room. I can hardly sit still. I am afraid my mother will wake up and afraid she won't. I sit opposite this stranger, wondering what she is thinking. Does she think I drove my mother to this? Does she think I might try to help my mother in her suicide attempt? Is she sympathetic or is she critical of this situation? Is she a friend or foe? I have no idea.

The clock reads 2:00 p.m. Thirty-four hours left.

"David, I have to get out of this room for a few moments," I plead.

I know that I have to discuss these new developments out from under the watchful eye of this nurse. I tell the nurse that we will be right outside at the end of the hall, and to please come get me if my mother's condition changes.

We are walking toward the end of the hall holding on to each other silently. I feel David's warmth against my frozen body. It feels comforting. I sit down on the cold marble sill and the reality of this chilling experience floods my body. The tears begin to flow again. I whisper, "Tell me what to do."

"You are doing all you can," David says. "Time will decide for you what will come next. You have to wait it out. You have to stand vigil and protect your mom."

"But maybe I need to save her, to do everything I can to bring her back. What if I am making a terrible mistake?" I cry. I know the answer before it is said.

"Your mother woke up to tell you what to do. You have to abide by her wishes now," my husband answers.

I turn away to look out at the world outside this window. The sky is still an icy white. There are no answers out there, only strangers. A city filled with people with their own tragedies, their own impossible discussions. Inside these walls there is still someone who feels my pain, someone who loves me and comforts me. I turn back to look into my husband's eyes. I fall into his lap sobbing. I remember my mother's words: "Never take your lover for granted. Your partner is everything." She always said she hated it when I fought with my husband. I truly understand now what she meant. What would I do without my David?

It was time to return to the room. Inside there is no change, only now the clock on the wall reads 2:30 p.m.

The next six long hours pass uneventfully. I sit by my mother's bedside waiting for something to happen, but nothing does. Most of the time David and I are silent. The nurse sits alone reading her newspaper. She only leaves to go to the bathroom, and when she does a floor nurse comes to relieve her. We are never alone. Occasionally other nurses come and check my mother's vital signs. I am beginning to crumble from exhaustion. By 9:30 p.m. my eyes close and I am asleep. The next thing I know I am awakened by the sunrise outside my mother's window.

I slowly focus on the clock. It is 6:30 a.m. Sixteen hours have passed since I held the receiver to my ear and heard the words, "You have thirty-six hours." My mother is still alive. She is still at death's door, but the door is still shut. She has not moved in all these hours.

I feel cold and clammy. I have been in the same clothes for what seems like days, and I have hardly eaten. My strength is waning. I must get a grip on myself because this day is crucial. I wash my face. The sting of the cold water revives my senses. We are still all here in this whitewashed room: my mother and I, David, and the nurse. Hours have passed; the clock ticks on, but nothing has changed.

David goes to get breakfast. He returns with hot coffee and bagels. I have no appetite, but I eat to save my strength. As the food enters my body, I feel as though each bite I take is a betrayal of my mother. I can't take another swallow. She is suffering—how can I eat? There is the sound of voices in the hall outside my mother's room. I peer outside and see that the doctors are beginning to make their rounds. I wonder when they will get to our room and what they will say and do.

The clock says 7:30 a.m. when they finally enter the room. It is the chief attending and two residents. He introduces them and then gives a full history of Steffi's condition. He asks if I would please leave the room so he can examine my mother, but I refuse. I am so afraid of what they might do to her. The doctor senses that I am not leaving the room under any circumstances, so he lets me stay. David leaves the room. As they begin to examine my mother's limp body, I see bruises all over her back.

"What happened?" I shriek in horror.

The doctor replies in a curt tone, "I think she must have fallen after she took all those pills."

I remember back to the apartment and the notes in the bathroom. She must have fallen in her desperate attempt to place those notes. My poor mother, how she had suffered. Now I wonder if she is in pain. I ask the doctor if she can feel pain in her comatose state, and he says he doesn't think so but he can't be sure.

Again he asks, "Don't you want us to do more to support her recovery?"

I can't answer. I don't know. I can sense his frustration with me. He abruptly turns to the other residents and says, "We are finished in this room. We can't do any more for Mrs. Mannheimer. Our hands are tied. Her daughter is opposed to any further treatment."

With that they turn toward the door and exit the room. David returns. He asks me what happened, but I have no words. I am numb. We sit in silence again.

Hours pass without the slightest movement of my mother's body. She is still turned away from the window; away from life outside these walls. All of a sudden it dawns on me: we are her protectors now. We are keeping watch so no one hurts Steffi anymore.

I am no longer confused. I know what I have to do and I feel stronger now. I am resolved that no one is going to touch my mother. I ask David to walk outside to the window at the end of the hall.

"David, I am resolved to shield my mother from any further harm. Seeing my mother's bruises has made me understand that she has suffered enough," I say. "I think I can handle this now. I am going to try my best. Please just be here to support me in whatever arises next."

David smiles and gives me a strong loving hug. "I'll be there for you, Evie," he says.

I know he will. My mother always called me Evie. As I sit on the windowsill, my mind wanders back in time to when David and I first fell in love. I was seventeen years old but knew then that our love would last a lifetime. I was supposed to leave for college the summer of 1967. I was secretly pinned to David in the spring, which was, at that time, a commitment before getting engaged. My mother found out by accident while cleaning up my room. I had left the pin on my nightstand. She was not very happy in those days with my choice of a life partner. David came from a middle class, blue-collar family. She had envisioned me marrying into royalty or old money. Somehow my mother thought she had given birth to a princess. In other words, my mother was a bit of a snob.

She came running into the kitchen shrieking, "What have you done? What does this pin mean?"

I said in a defiant, self-confident tone, "I'm pinned to David. We love each other and there is nothing you can do about it."

With that she did an about-face and stomped down the hall into her bedroom and slammed the door. I should have known better, but I was young and hell bent on stating my independence. So I followed her right back into her bedroom. She looked at me in a panic.

"You are throwing your whole life away and I will not have it!" she yelled.

With that my mother climbed up onto the windowsill and threatened to jump if I didn't return the pin. I looked at her smugly and said, "So jump." I knew that, even though we were three stories above the street, there was an archway over the front door of the apartment building right under the bedroom window. If she'd jumped she would have only dropped eighteen inches.

Over the years my mother grew to love my husband. I suppose she felt she was leaving me in good hands now.

It is time to return to the room. I have left Mom alone long enough and I don't trust that nurse. I trust no one in this hospital. I sit back down next to my mother with a new understanding of my role in all of this.

There is a knock on the door. I turn to see another stranger entering my mother's room. She smiles and introduces herself as the hospital social worker. She asks if there is anything she can do. She has heard about my mother's unfortunate situation and she would like to help if she can. Her kind words seem out of place in what has become a cold and hostile environment. Can I trust this stranger? As we begin to talk, my back is turned away from my mother. Suddenly the social worker motions to me to turn around. I look back at my mother. Her eyes are open and she is crying. She can't speak but she is motioning to me to come closer. I am trembling, fighting back my tears.

"Talk to her," the social worker says. "Say what is in your heart."

"I forgive you, Mommy. I forgive you." I can't manage to say anymore.

The social worker encourages me again. "This is your chance to make peace, to say things that some people never get a chance to say."

I begin again and I tell her she has been a good mother and a good grandmother and that it is all right. That I understand. That I know she has suffered and that I am here for her. My mother holds out her frail hand. I take it and in a whisper she says, "Evie, I love you so."

I squeeze her hand tight. I am filled with so many emotions: anger, sorrow, and deep love. I stroke her head and kiss her forehead. I speak softly into her ear, "I love you too. It's all right, you can let go now. I forgive you. I understand."

The social worker says again, "If there is anything else you want to say, say it now." But there is nothing left to say. Those four words, "I love you so," say it all. My mother's eyes are closed again. She is in a deep sleep. In my heart I know this will be our last conversation. We have forgiven each other. Mommy and I have made peace and the nurse, the social worker, and my dear husband have borne witness. It is a divine moment and I know a greater power than us has lent a hand and intervened.

Steffi is sleeping soundly. Her face is relaxed. I feel a strong sense of resolve now. I am here to protect Mommy. My last duty as a daughter is to sit vigil at her bedside and to make sure no one disturbs her as she slips peacefully farther and farther away from life.

There is nothing left to do but wait. Hour after hour passes without change. I begin to panic again. What if the deadline passes? What if the doctors intervene? What will I do?

It is 7:30 p.m. By morning the deadline will have passed and I will have to deal with the doctors once again. I am exhausted. I need to go home and rest so I can face tomorrow. I know no one will touch her till tomorrow.

The nurse encourages me to go home. She says, "I will call you if anyone comes in or if there is any change." I don't want to leave, but I have no more strength left and I know I will need all my faculties to confront the doctors in the morning. I finally agree to go home for a short rest. I take Steffi's hand, kiss her forehead once again, and whisper, "I love you Mommy" into her ear. She does not respond.

As I leave the room, I am overcome by a strange sense of loneliness, as if my mother has already passed away. In a sense she has. I am never going to speak to her again. She will never hold my hand or hug me. She will never say "I love you so" again. But in my mind I will hear those words over and over again forever. Every time I look up into the heavens, I will hear her.

We are in the car driving away from the hospital. The clock in the car reads 9:36 p.m. My cell phone rings. The voice on the other end says, "Your mother is gone. She passed peacefully at half past nine."

CHAPTER 6

Visiting Jeff

It is a late icy blue February sky. One month has melted away with the winter snow since Mommy passed away. But the memories are still so vivid. The days bleed into each other until I can no longer remember what day it really is.

My husband has gone back to work and I sit alone again in my kitchen as time passes slowly on. I worry about my children and what this tragedy has done to them. Eden has gone back to medical school. I am not sure where her strength is coming from. I worry daily about her mental state. How is she coping with all that has happened? She has great strength, but she is counting on me to guide her and help her understand why her grandmother took her own life and left us with all this guilt. Eden has been my rock, but now it is my turn to be her support. She has so much in front of her and she is very much alone. Eden has chosen such a difficult path for herself. I must try to be her strength now.

My son, Jeff, has gone back to college after saying goodbye to Grandma Steffi and attending her funeral. I was so numb at the time that I hardly felt or remembered his or anyone else's presence in my mother's hospital room or at her funeral.

At least I know he is in a solid relationship and that this will help him. I console myself with this thought, but I feel so helpless; so out of control. For him the distance is both good and bad. He is shielded from some of this terrible pain, but he is also the outsider looking in on this family tragedy from a far place. How will that affect him? I wonder. He loved his grandma. I decide that I should visit my son. I need to gather whatever strength I have left and go and see Jeff.

As I drive the four-hour ride up to Ithaca, NY through the small towns of Pennsylvania and then into New York, memories of my childhood come racing back with each mile I travel. I have journeyed these roads many times before my children ever started their college days at Cornell University. I remember driving up to Syracuse University, the college I attended from 1967–1970, for the first time. We stopped on the Cornell campus on the way to Syracuse, NY. We had lunch in Willard Strait on the west campus. I commented on how beautiful the school was and my mother sarcastically retorted, "Well Evie, if you had applied yourself a little more when you were at Music and Art High School, you could be attending school here instead of Syracuse."

Those words stung like a wasp bite. I have never forgotten that moment. I wasn't good enough again. How ironic that my two children should have picked this university to attend.

As I ride by the small towns of Dryden and Lisle on Route 79, it begins to snow during the last forty-five minutes of my trip. I remember trudging through the snow on my way to class in my college days with my portfolio and my long hair blowing in the wind and covering my face. I was an art student filled with very liberal ideas in those days. I marched against the Vietnam War, much to my mother's disapproval. I wanted to be nothing like her. I wanted the freedom to think for myself. I had no idea in those days how much more my mother knew about life than I did. I was too busy trying to be different than her to find out.

Now that I look back on her critical advice, I realize how much truth was in her words. I could have tried harder, and I could have been more focused.

I am at the entrance to west campus. It is snowing quite hard now and I have to find Jeff. I am here to help him through this sad time, but I know that seeing him will be a great comfort to me. Jeff reminds me so much of myself when I was his age. He is filled with the spirit of adventure. I understand that life has made me much more cautious now. My mother's constant threats of suicide wore away my sense of optimism.

As I approach the street where Jeff lives, a sense of desperation grips me. What will I say to my son? What words can I say? I arrive at his apartment just as the day is slipping away. It is 4:30 p.m. Just seeing his face is a lifeline to me. "I have my children. There is still family. We love each other. We will help each other," I tell myself.

I cannot control the tears. One by one they drip from my eyes even though I am trying so hard to suppress them. Jeff is hugging me now and I have nothing but gratitude for this moment. I am so thankful for this son of mine. Instead of a child who needs comfort, a man stands before me strong and sympathetic.

Jeff and I agree that I will check into the hotel and then I will pick him up for dinner. I am concerned over the weather, but he lets me know that we will be fine. I have trouble believing that anything will ever be fine again. But just being on this campus with my son is a sign of hope.

I check into the Best Western where I have spent many weekends during my children's Cornell days. Just a half a year ago my mother had been here with me for Eden's graduation from college. She had been so proud of her granddaughter. The hills of Cornell had been hard for my mother to negotiate. I had been impatient with her. I was resentful that such a special moment in my life was being compromised by her handicaps. I never really realized how much physical and mental anguish she must have been in. Now I am so glad she had that proud moment to be Eden Rauch's grandmother. She had finally gotten her Ivy League graduate.

I am picking up Jeff for dinner. It is about 7:00 p.m. There is frost forming on my windshield, and the snow is falling lightly creating a white blanket over the campus. It is so beautiful and peaceful. We are on our way to our favorite Ithaca restaurant, John Thomas Steakhouse. We have celebrated many happy occasions at John Thomas. My mother had been there during Eden's graduation weekend. It seems fitting that Jeff and I should be here now. Although this is not a happy occasion, it is an important one. Jeff had made a reservation, and they seat us immediately, across from a wood burning fireplace that gives a warm glow to the room. The restaurant still has some Christmas decorations adorning the fireplace and the doorways. It feels good to relax for a moment. I had not dared to let down my guard since I was summoned to my mother's apartment.

My son's sense of humor and his sensitivity to my vulnerable state is so endearing. He tries so hard to be sympathetic and caring. We have had our differences in these past several years, but for this moment in time there is no awkwardness about our conversation. We are talking about Grandma Steffi and how, even though she had infuriated us at times, we loved her and missed her.

Jeff is telling me that he wishes he had spent more time with her. That he should have visited her at her home when he came home for his college breaks. I tell him that we are all going to feel we could have done more, said more, and helped more. But in truth, she had pushed us away a lot. Her illness had overwhelmed her in a cloud of depression, and she was incapable of receiving kindness gracefully.

"We all did the best we could, given the circumstances," I tell him. "She loved her grandchildren so much, but her illness played a cruel trick on her and she lost the weapons to fight her uphill battle. In the end she just gave up and thought everyone would be better off without her. I failed to make her see that that was not the truth. But it is too late for self-incrimination," I say. "We just need to love each other and love her memory. And never forget her. She would want us to be close and to be happy."

We eat our juicy steaks and top off the meal with a brownie sundae. I stare at my adult son and recognize that I must have done something right. He is a fine young man. No more the defiant little rascal he used to be. Mom was right. She always told me he would turn out all right. We get the check and head out into the night. The snow is coming down heavily now. It is hard to see out of the car windshield.

All the time we are driving Jeff keeps telling me that we'll be all right. I begin to believe him. How could anything ruin this evening? I am so glad I came to see my son. I know he will be fine, and I hope I will be too. Soon Jeff will be graduating from this prestigious university. I wish Mom could have held out to witness Jeff's graduation, but somehow I know she will be there in the crowd cheering her grandson on. With all her pessimism, she believed in Jeff and loved him so.

CHAPTER 7

Riding Back in Time

It is March 20th. My anniversary. There will be no celebrations this year. Two months have gone by since I saw my mother for the last time. I am in the kitchen unable to open the door to the garage. My hand will not grab the doorknob. I feel a deep pain in the pit of my stomach, the acid is backing up into my throat, and I can hardly breathe. The sour taste of my anguish is making me nauseous. I must be on my way. I will be late, but I can't seem to grab the doorknob.

It is a cold, gray day, not unlike the days I spent in the hospital as my mother passed slowly from life to death. Not unlike the day I picked up the phone and a stranger spoke the words, "Are you Steffi Mannheimer's daughter? You better come to your mother's apartment quickly. I think your mother is in deep trouble. There are notes." I've spent these months basically in seclusion trying to grasp the fact that my mother is gone. The emptiness is deep, and the silence deafening.

There are no more late night desperate cries for help. No more sadistic, critical remarks said when my mother's health was failing. But there also would be no more phone calls asking how my day went, what was I doing, or could I come to the city? Letting me know she missed me and wanted to spend time. Those conversations you only have with your mother. The one's about the deep love she had for me and my family. How her grandchildren and I were her whole life. The person who loved me most in the whole world is gone.

I grab the doorknob and slam the door behind me. I am out of the house. The frigid weather gives me the chills as I quickly slide into the driver's seat of my car. I have one last moment of hesitation then I turn the ignition key.

My car knows the way almost by itself. It is a good thing because I am barely concentrating on the road. This time I am traveling alone. My daughter is back in medical school finishing her first year. My mind wanders back to the last time I traveled this path. Eden had been with me, she had been my rock. Now I will have to rely on myself. I turn on the traffic report. There seem to be no tie-ups. It will take about an hour and a half to reach my mother's apartment house. The ride seems longer than ever before. This will probably be the last time I will ever make this trip.

I remember back to when I first moved to New Jersey. My mother was against it. She wanted me to be closer to New York. She would always say, "How could you move to such a location in the sticks?" But as the years passed she grew to love my home and the rural countryside. She rarely complained about making a trip out to see me and the family even though she traveled on three buses to get to us, and the trip took two and a half hours. She loved to see her grandchildren.

Eden was the apple of her eye, mostly because they shared a love for music. Eden started playing the violin at six. My mother delighted in her accomplishments, and for Eden's thirteenth birthday she bought her a very special, expensive, vintage violin. It had the most beautiful rich tone when Eden played it.

My thoughts drift back to a lovely day my mother, Eden, and I spent at the Metropolitan Opera seeing *Carmen* many years ago. Mom loved the elegant atmosphere at the Met. She invited us to lunch on the second tier of the opera house, and we ate the main course before the opera and had dessert during intermission. I remember ordering strawberries, raspberries, and cream, my father's favorite. Eden had chocolate cake and my mother had apple strudel. She never liked gooey cakes as she put it. It was as if we were in the opera house in

Vienna, Austria. Eden, nine at the time, was on her best behavior. She wore white lace gloves, as did Grandma Steffi. Three generations of women sharing an afternoon of culture and love. We laughed about the overdramatic acting of the star performers. I had wished I had the appreciation for music that they had, but I never quite developed their same affection for classical music. After that, my mother took Eden to the opera without me several times. But now as my taste in music has matured, I can appreciate the happiness that Steffi derived from listening to classical music for hours. It was in a concert hall that she felt most at home. Her sweetest memories were all tied up in the music from her childhood.

I glance at the car clock. It is 12:45 p.m. I am nearing the George Washington Bridge. The times I have crossed over this bridge into New York are too numerous to count. Many times I was hurrying to see my mother who was in some kind of emergency. But there were happier occasions, too. One of my last pleasant visits was on her birthday, November 16th, just two months before she died. I picked her up at her apartment and crossed back over the George Washington Bridge heading back to New Jersey. It was a cold, sunny day. The bridge was shining and the water below sparkling. We had lunch in a place close to the bridge that had seen better days, but inside it was jumping. There were two wedding showers going on, and there were quite a few patrons although the place was not full by any means.

For the first time in years we actually talked and really enjoyed each other's company. We talked about old times when my father was alive. We talked about my grandmother and how we missed her. And we talked about my kids, who she so loved. Jeff in particular always had a special spot in her heart, and she felt I was too hard on him. She had wanted a son herself. Jeff was the only boy in the family. We stayed there for three hours. Neither she nor I wanted to leave.

Our meal was mediocre, but my mother seemed to enjoy it. She smiled and actually ate her whole lunch. It was some kind of meat smothered in gravy. My mother always liked to eat wet food—it was easier for her to swallow. I had a salad, which she criticized. "That is for rabbits," she snapped. But she did not harp on it that time. It was just a passing comment. I ordered a piece of cake and a candle for her birthday and the waiter sang to her. Because of her facial paralysis she could not blow the candle out. I had to help her. Her facial paralysis did not give her enough breath to blow it out. Her face saddened, and I felt sorry that I had embarrassed her. She began to talk about how I would be fine without her and that it was time for her to go. I tried to tell her that I loved her and needed her, but I sensed that she was not listening. She changed the subject. We ate the cake and she seemed happier. All in all, I felt we had a good afternoon.

I am on the upper level of the George Washington Bridge heading toward New York and my mother's apartment. I look across at Manhattan. I remember crossing the bridge to take my mom home. How majestic the bridge is. I had never really paid attention to the beauty of this part of the ride. I hear my mom telling me one afternoon on the deck at home, "You run so much, Evie. You never take time to smell the roses. You should sit outside in your garden and just admire your garden." At the time I had taken it as just another criticism of me and how I lived my life. But now it seems like solid advice. It was in her delivery that I always felt demoralized and angry. I never seemed to do the right thing although I felt I was trying so hard. But I did not take time to stop and look at my surroundings. I was always running somewhere. I had a full life and little time to waste, but I could take a moment to see the beauty that surrounded me.

I cross the bridge and drive toward the Henry Hudson Parkway. To my left is Columbia Presbyterian Hospital where my mother had her surgery to remove a benign acoustic neuroma. The day before my mother's brain surgery in 1982, David and I were sitting in her room at the hospital. The surgeon had not indicated that there would be any problems removing her tumor and had given her a very optimistic prognosis. My mom was very agitated. In her tough Germanic manner, she ordered me to make sure that if she was handicapped in any way from the surgery, I would tell the doctors to let her die. I told her that I could not do that. They would do their best and she would be all right. There was no reason to believe otherwise. She became irate and screamed, "Promise me you won't let me be handicapped! Promise me." I could not calm her down. Finally she stopped and asked us to leave. That was the last time I saw my mother as a whole person.

Her surgery took twelve hours. When I was finally able to see her, it was obvious that something had gone terribly wrong. She was not fit for life when she woke up from that surgery. Her doctor never came to talk to us. He sent the resident who could barely look me in the eye as he told us how her benign tumor was close to the brain stem, and somehow some cranial nerves were cut and caused the paralysis. He wasn't sure exactly what had happened. The poor resident was shaking as he described her condition. Her surgeon was nowhere to be found.

I'm on the ramp to the parkway now. I recall the day we took Steffi home from her brain surgery. My husband was driving. My mother was inconsolable. Mom was paralyzed on the left side of her face and throat. Her saliva dripped out of the side of her mouth, and because she had no gag reflex on the left side, she was constantly choking on her saliva. It made eating virtually impossible. She was terribly disfigured. Her balance was poor and she had trouble walking. Her eyesight was altered as the eyelid on the left side was paralyzed. She was also deaf in the left ear. She was truly suffering.

She began to shout at me, badgering me, "I told you to let me die. This is your entire fault, Evie. I do not want to live this way. You can't make me. I hate you for doing this to me..." and on and on and on. David abruptly stopped the car on the ramp, opened her door, and told her to get out. I became hysterical. But he was serious. He had had enough and she knew it. She stopped talking, and not another word was spoken that day.

From that day forward her life was a living nightmare, and our family lived that nightmare along with her. We saw every specialist we could for every problem that had occurred from her original unsuccessful surgery. She had five operations, from several plastic surgeries to eye surgery to help diminish her discomfort; but no one could truly restore what she had lost. Her bitterness continued to deepen, and the tension between us was ever present. I was trying to save a woman who did not want to be saved.

My car clock reads 1:15. Fifteen more minutes and I should be at my mother's apartment; the home I grew up in. I am on the parkway now, passing the Cloisters, a park in upper Manhattan. I used to come here when I was a little girl still in a stroller, when my family was whole; my father was alive and hadn't yet had his first heart attack at forty-five-years-old. That was when my parents still loved each other; before illness destroyed their relationship and their lives. The park was beautiful in those days. We had picnics there and my father would laugh and tease me. Whatever my father said, I always believed him. He was so convincing and funny. I adored him then. He was so handsome and he made everything fun. He was such a practical joker. Jeff is so much like my father. It is sad that they never got to meet each other.

I am sitting in my car in front of Steffi's apartment building now trying to decide if I have the strength to face packing up her belongings alone. I told David that I needed to do this by myself, but now that I am here I'm not sure I have made the right choice. I open the car door and stand up, take a deep breath and walk toward the building.

For so many of my growing up years I had taken this same walk. Now it would be for the last time. Through the courtyard I enter the front door of the building and go into the lobby, which is dark and smells stale. This is my past not my future, I think. I get to the elevator and the memory of being stuck in it so many times comes back to me so I decide to take the stairs. The staircase is steep and the three flights of stairs take my breath away. I wonder how my mother ever made it up these stairs. She was one tough lady. She rarely carried a cane even though she really could have used one. Her pride was too strong—she was determined to do everything alone, and that was her strength as well as her weakness. In the end she even orchestrated her own death alone. But her decision to go it alone all the time often ended up with disastrous outcomes and consequences involving the very people she had tried so hard to exclude. I suppose she deluded herself in believing that she was protecting her family. Somehow it never turned out that way. She needed assistance much of the time and her refusal of my help and resentment toward me made it difficult, because in the end she needed and had to accept my assistance. I became unsympathetic as a result. Taking care of Steffi became an obligation rather than a labor of love. Although I loved my mother deeply, I couldn't figure her out and I suffered right along with her.

I am at the door to her apartment. 3H. The hallway walls are painted a medium shade of blue and there is dim lighting from a single bulb in the ceiling. My hands are trembling and numb. I turn the key and the cylinder clicks open, but I can't grab the doorknob. I feel paralyzed. What will I find in this Pandora's box? Fear grabs me by the throat and I feel the bile churning in my stomach. I want to run from this place. Run far, far away. I want to wake up from this nightmare. But it is not a dream; far from it. Finally the blood returns to my hands and I turn the doorknob to enter the apartment. It is dark and still; no sweet classical music, which used to emanate from my mother's apartment. Only silence.

CHAPTER 8

The Apartment

I turn on the light in the foyer. The first thing I see is the front closet. I open it cautiously. In it are an assortment of coats and hats. My mother always wanted a fur coat but she never bought one, just a fur-lined raincoat that she wore whenever the weather turned cold and inclement. In winter she invariably wore a scarf, hat, and gloves. She was meticulous about her appearance. She wore coordinating jewelry and accessories with whatever outfit she was wearing. She wore heels even though her balance was poor after her surgery. My mother refused to give in and took many tumbles. The paralysis of the left side of her face was particularly devastating to her because she had always been interested in fashion. My father was a dress salesman, and for years after his death my mother continued his business. In later years she worked at Saks Fifth Avenue in the coat department. I remember wanting to pay her a surprise visit at Saks one afternoon when I was in the city with David. We took the escalator to the fourth floor coat department expecting to see her helping a customer. Instead the manager told us that she was at the doctor and he had been instructed by her not to let anyone know why. I ran to a pay phone to call my mother. That was the day I found out she had a brain tumor.

There are two canes in the closet. I very rarely saw my mother with one of these. She only used them when the weather was very bad and she had to leave the house, or when she was feeling very unsteady. She was a proud German woman, even though she thought of herself just as an American citizen. She would tell my grandmother to speak English because they were Americans now and not Germans. But her German heritage was ever present in all of her being. She could not escape her past even though she tried hard to.

I walk farther into the apartment. In front of me is the dining area. My mother was a wonderful cook, but she rarely let me help her in the kitchen. I learned most of my cooking skills on my own. She was very nervous when I entered the kitchen, and I in turn felt that way when she tried to help me in my kitchen. But on rare occasions she would let me help, and I would feel proud to have had a part in preparing a beautiful and sumptuous meal. I have fond memories of the holidays at home. The house would be abuzz with activity, and I remember my mother singing while she cooked. She loved to entertain. Her dining room table was impeccably set with china and stemware and silverware. There was always a beautiful arrangement of flowers on the table.

I was an only child as was my mother. My father had a brother and two sisters and they shared the holidays with us. My mother tried so hard to assimilate herself into my father's family, but they never gave her a break. They were relentlessly critical of her and she felt alienated and alone. Only my aunt, Babette, who had a softness and gentleness about her, was genuinely kind to my mother and me. I suspect the rest of the bunch was jealous of my mother since they were all childless and many years older than she.

My grandmother, Kathe, was a formidable presence. She would add balance to the family table. As long as she was around, my father's family would be on their best behavior. Everyone liked my grandmother, but they feared her a little as well. My grandmother couldn't cook, so she made a big fuss over my mother's cooking. That also created tension between my mother and my father's family. To make matters worse, my father would always complain that there was too much food prepared and the Mannheimer family would whole-heartedly agree.

But the holidays were still joyous. I would be allowed to stay up late and have dessert. Steamed chocolate pudding with vanilla sauce was my all-time favorite. I begged my mother to make it. It was a lot of work. Something could go wrong and the whole pudding could deflate. It was like a light soufflé but cooked in a water bath. It had to be timed just right. It was made with bitter sweet chocolate but it was not overly sweet. The richness of the vanilla sauce was a delicious compliment. I guess because it took so much delicate preparation it was special and the whole family loved it.

I never knew what I was missing by not having other siblings around. I was alone a lot of the time, but there were perks to being an only child. I got away with a lot of mischief and I was quite spoiled. Every holiday Aunt Babette would bring me chocolate, nonpareils from a German candy store on Eighty-Sixth Street. She would always include Aunt Rosel, my father's other sister, when she gave it to me; but I knew she had bought them. Whenever I am in that neighbor-hood I look for that store and buy some nonpareils. It tastes better than any other chocolate I have ever eaten.

After my father died, Aunt Rosel gave me a bracelet that my fa-ther had made for her during his time in the army. It was the only thing she ever gave me herself, but it means a lot to me now.

Beyond the dining area to the right and two steps down is the liv-ing room. I walk straight toward it, avoiding the hall to the bedroom. I remember the first time David came to see my parents. We sat in this living room. There is candy on the table as if my mother is wait-ing for company to come. But in the past several years there had been few guests. A lot of my mother's friends had died or moved away or were too old and frail to make visits anymore.

The living room has a real elegance about it. David and I had our wedding reception in this apartment. My parents had wanted to give us a formal wedding in June of 1970, but my father suffered a serious heart attack in January of that year. After much discussion it was decided that we would move up the date to March, have the ceremony in the rabbi's study, and the reception at the apartment. My mother was heartbroken over the decision. She had looked forward to the wedding of her only daughter for years. That dream was over and I had to put my foot down for Steffi to understand that we'd made the right decision; so many of her dreams had not come true. But she came around to see that there was really no choice. We told my father that the money for the wedding would be better spent on giving us a start toward our future and he agreed. He must have known how sick he was but he played along.

My mother made a beautiful reception for us. Everything from the delicious food and fine table linens to the beautiful flowers reflected her classy style. We only had our parents and my grandmother and a few close friends at the reception. Curiously, my mother insisted on inviting Gerry Goldsmith, a distant cousin of my mother's and a wealthy real-estate investor. I had visited Gerry several times while I was growing up. He had taken an interest in me and I think my mother and grandmother had hoped that someday he would introduce me to a wealthy man who would become my husband. It was strange to have him included on such a small guest list. But my mother insisted. Altogether I think there were fifteen people. We were happy and we celebrated. On May 24th of that year my father died—twelve days before my original wedding date and two months before my twenty-first birthday. Instead of wedding plans, we were making funeral arrangements and sitting shiva.

There is a rosewood and chrome breakfront in the living room. It was very modern in the 1960s and still looks beautiful. It has glass doors and behind them the only valuable possessions my mother owned are displayed. There is a cigarette holder disguised as a silver and gold globe. My father smoked three packs a day, the probable cause of his early death at sixty-one. As I open the globe, I remember the day I came home from my first summer at sleep-away camp. It was a Friday morning. My father had to work, and so my mother picked me up alone from the camp bus. I was sitting in my room playing and about one o'clock in the afternoon the doorbell rang. My mother shouted from her bedroom, "Evie, go answer the door. I bet it is your father. He came home early to surprise you." I ran, happy and excited, to the door and flung it open expecting my father to yell surprise and give me a huge hug. But instead the surprise was that he fell in on me. He was having his first of many heart attacks.

My mother came down the hall from the bedroom expecting to see my father and me happy to be reunited after a fun-filled summer. Instead, total panic set in. Somehow we got him to the bedroom and onto the bed. I sat in the corner of the bedroom for what seemed like hours, not moving a muscle or uttering a word. My mother took charge. She called the police and tried to keep my father calm until the paramedics arrived. She told me to go to my room and stay on my bed till she said I could come out. I was so afraid that my father was dying that I listened without protest. I lay on my bed sobbing as the paramedics wheeled my father out and down the hall on a stretcher. That is all I remember. I was seven-years-old at the time.

As I look farther through the breakfront glass, I see a cut crystal vase. I recall flowers being delivered every year on my mother's birthday. Twenty-four red roses every year like clockwork. They were not from my father, as I was told by my grandmother many years after his death. My mother had been in love with her best friend's father, and for several years had fantasized about running away with him. My grandmother had put a stop to the whole affair by threatening to ruin the man financially. Soon after that my mother met my father. But the other man, a father figure, a replacement for the father she barely knew, was really her only true love; she never consummated it. My father never once questioned where the flowers came from. I guess he didn't want to know, or maybe he knew already and didn't have to ask. One year the flowers stopped coming.

There is a lovely large, modern silver bowl. My parents bought it on a trip we took to Mexico. As I hold this bowl and look into it, I see my reflection and the memory of all the trips my parents took me on stares back at me. The wonderful trips to Europe, the national parks in this country, the Caribbean, and Mexico. I had forgotten those happy times. My parents loved to travel. I remember being very young and skipping down the street with my mother across the Ponte Vecchio bridge in Florence, Italy. I was embarrassed by her silly behavior. She had had a couple of glasses of wine with dinner and was in a giddy mood. It was so rare that I saw my mother happy and playful. I didn't know how to react to it. But there was a side to my mother that she rarely showed; a hidden desire to be a joyous, free spirit. Those trips were the happiest times of my childhood. My father and mother would put aside their differences and we would have a wonderful holiday. I danced with father on my eighteenth birthday on the terrace at the Villa d'Este in Lake Como, Italy. He was a wonderful dancer and I felt like a princess.

Everything was so elegant when we traveled. My parents were not rich by any means, but when they traveled, they traveled in style. For a moment in time the clock stopped ticking and we were a happy family. I will always cherish those memories of my vacations with Mommy and Daddy. I will treasure this bowl for its reflection.

Inside the breakfront, behind closed doors, are the dishes that my mother used for all her wonderful dinner parties. The flecks of gold that lined the border of the plates are barely visible now. There is silver flatware in a drawer lined with felt. The silver has lost its luster from decades of use. The pattern is simple, straight line elegance. Together they were so beautiful on Steffi's table. We had bought them many years ago, when I was thirteen, on a trip to Germany in a posh store in Frankfurt. It was the first time my mother and father had gone back to visit their former homeland. I remember this trip vividly even though I was young because it was bittersweet for my parents, and the only trip in my memory that was not so joyous.

My mother had a cousin still living in Germany. She had survived the war because her mother had married a Christian and converted. Mariana, my mother's cousin, had been raised Christian. Even so, she and her mother had been in a work camp during the war and had been treated badly. The Nuremburg Laws proposed by Hitler and adopted by the German government on September 15, 1935 stated that even converts and children of mixed blood were not considered part of the Aryan race, and therefore were enemies of the state. My grandmother and my mother had paid for Mariana to come to the United States to visit several times. She had been very jealous of my mother and made her feel guilty that we had a higher living standard than she did and that my mother had escaped the camps. So every year my grandmother and my mother would send money for the holidays. Meanwhile, Mariana was living in a better style then they were, as my mother found out on our visit.

Mariana took us shopping at the largest and most fashionable department store in Frankfurt. My mother asked a sales lady to show her a sweater that was in one of the glass cases. She spoke to her in German. I was able to understand the conversation because I had heard German spoken in my home growing up even though my mother never encouraged me to learn German. The sales lady refused to help my mother, telling her that the sweater wouldn't fit her. I had spoken to my mother in English and the woman had figured out that we were visitors. The sales lady surmised that my mother was Jewish because she had an American-born child and an older German dialect. I could see the tears form in my mother's eyes. That was the first of several anti-Semitic encounters we would have on that trip.

After our visit with Mariana in Frankfurt, we continued our travels in Germany. I remember having lunch in a small restaurant in the countryside. My father was excited because he had ordered wild strawberries, something he had loved as a child growing up in Germany. When they came, he said they didn't quite taste the same. He had been looking for those strawberries for years everywhere we went. "I guess what you remember is never quite the same in reality," my mother and I teased him. As we sat laughing together about the strawberry controversy, a man at the next table struck up a conversation with my father. He was a bit older than my father, graying around the temples and slightly overweight. He started joking with my father. I could see that my father was preoccupied with something as he continued to converse with the friendly gentleman. All of a sudden my father abruptly ended the conversation, got the check, and hastily hurried us out of the café.

My father was ashen. He told us that he recognized the man, although he was older, as a Gestapo officer in the labor camp my father was in back in 1936. We never returned to Germany. Several times my mother visited Europe alone after my father died, but she would always meet Mariana in another country.

As I look away from the breakfront, I see the large, depressing painting that hangs over my mother's couch. I was in my late twenties when my mother purchased that painting. I was the artist in the family and she never consulted me before she bought the painting. I remember feeling terribly hurt every time I saw the painting. She never valued my opinion, I thought. Even though this is my field of expertise, she still did not trust me to know enough. The painting overshadows the room and creates a depressing atmosphere that wasn't present when I grew up in this apartment or when I got married in this room. My mother regretted the purchase of the painting, and several years ago told me she was sorry she ever bought it. In her last note to me she said, "Make money from everything. Keep what you want and sell the rest." I know I will sell this painting someday. It is a sad reminder of Steffi and my regrets.

I imagine that I will give the furniture to Eden if she wants it. With a little creative refurbishing it will look as good as new and be a lovely gift from my mother to her granddaughter. Eden will be moving into her own apartment soon. I can put all these things in storage for a while. It just all seems so overwhelming. How do you pack up someone's whole life?

I move from the living room up the two steps into the hall. I pause for a moment. It is so hard to retrace these steps. I have walked down this hall all my life, always fearing that someday it would come to this moment. And here I am standing in the hall, afraid to move, afraid to say goodbye; afraid to close this chapter of my life. I have dreamed about this day, dreaded it, and at times wished for it. Now I feel only despair, sadness, and regret.

I move slowly down the hall. I enter my mother's bedroom. Everything is as it was. No one has been here since Eden and I left the apartment two months ago. The bed is unmade; the suitcase that my mother had half-packed sits on what was my father's bed. The closet doors are open. There are two dresser drawers pulled open. There are stains on the carpet. It feels as if Steffi should have returned to clean this up. This should not be my job. I can't do this job.

How could you do this to me, mommy, I think. How could you leave this to me? I remember the note in the bathroom. "Call my daughter. She will take care of everything." She trusted that I would.

I look closer. My mother told me a long time ago that she kept a beige sequined handbag of money in the closet. The bag is sitting on the dresser now, but when I look inside the money is gone. I imagine that either the police or the cleaning girl or the super found the bag, took advantage of the situation, and helped themselves. I hope it brought some happiness into their lives. It had not done that for my mother.

There is an open jewelry box on the dresser. My mother's gold bracelet is missing but her diamond engagement ring is still there. Whoever helped themselves to her money and her jewelry must have overlooked it, thinking it was costume jewelry. It has two emeralds missing that flanked the sides of a round diamond. The ring is dirty and misshapen. I had not seen it on my mother's hand since my father died. My grandmother had smuggled the diamond out of Nazi Germany. It had been the one precious thing she had escaped with. My father had no money for a ring, so she gave the stone to him and he designed the ring and had it made. Curiously, although it is in disrepair, it has such a simple elegance about it.

There is another small white box inside the jewelry box. At first it seems as though there is nothing in it—just a piece of cotton. But underneath the cotton is a large aquamarine ring. I remember this was the first important piece of jewelry my father ever bought my mother. It was on our first trip to Europe. I was very young but I still remember it.

We went into a small, exclusive jewelry store in Geneva. My mother was excited. She had always wanted an aquamarine, her favorite stone. I thought at the time it was the most beautiful ring I had ever seen. So rarely in my life had I witnessed my mother so blissfully happy. It is just a rock, but it represents something more. It was a special gift, an extravagance from a man who so rarely lavished my mother with anything. She loved that single piece of jewelry because of its beauty and because my father had wanted to buy it for her. I am glad that it went unnoticed. I will cherish this piece and remember what it represents—a happier moment in my life. How coincidental that it should be Eden's birth stone. Someday, God willing, it will be hers.

As I look farther into the jewelry box I find another ring, the only one my mother wore every day: three topaz squares set in a modern rectangular gold setting. I put it on my index finger and warmth flows through my hand. I can feel my mother's touch. I never saw my mother without this ring. I will never take this ring off. There is so little left of my mother in her earlier years, but I can always look down at my hand and remember an elegant lady. I pack up a few other belongings in the half-packed suitcase, zip it up, and carry it out of Steffi's bedroom.

CHAPTER 9

My Bedroom

A few steps away, across the hall, is the bedroom I grew up in. My mother had made it into a guest room/office, but my childhood dressers and desk are still there; and the three-colored cone lamp that my father hung for me when we moved in more than forty-five years ago still hangs in the middle of the room. The stereo that David and I bought many years ago and installed for my mother sits silent. There had always been music in this house, even when times were sad. Now there is only a defining silence.

I open the closet door and find a painting of a young girl. She is dressed in an old-fashioned lace collared dress and the painting seems to be very old. It has no signature and I have no idea who this could be. My mother had been so secretive, never wanting to look at the past. She never shared stories about her youth. I suppose I never really asked too many questions. Now it was too late to get her answers. I wonder if I will ever know who this young woman is in the painting, or will it remain a mystery forever?

I open the top drawer to my dresser expecting to find the past season's clothing, but instead there are papers, photographs, and documents filling the drawer. I freeze, unable to believe what I am seeing. I can tell from my scant knowledge of German that many of these documents are official papers from when my mother, father, and grandmother fled Nazi Germany. And there are letters written in my mother's own hand in German from 1939 and 1940. There are old photographs of family members long passed on. There are old cookbooks written by hand in German dated 1939. My hands are shaking as I fumble through the many folders in this drawer. These papers and photographs had been in my room for over thirty years just waiting to be discovered. Here alone in my room, which had been such an unhappy place for me for much of my childhood, hidden in my own dresser are the answers to why. My whole body is trembling now. I want to read every shred of paper in this drawer, but I can't. I am frustrated with my faltering German. Only some words are familiar. If only I had made an effort to learn how to read German growing up and asked more questions of my parents.

What will I do with all these documents? How will I begin to unravel the thread that links me to my past? I have no idea where this newly discovered information will take me or how I will use it to go forward. I know somehow the answer will come to me. I was meant to find these papers. They were left in my own top dresser drawer. My mother wanted me all along to find them someday, and today is that day.

I was meant to repent for my lack of understanding and to forgive, most of all to love, the family that these documents and letters are about. My mother left me a gift—a window into the past. She always said to me, "Knowledge is the key to every door. What you have in your head no one can ever take away from you."

The Ten Commandments teach us to honor our mothers and fathers. Here was a chance to honor my mother's memory in some way. I sit down on the couch in my room. I am not sure how to move forward from here. I want time to stand still. I am not ready for the clock to tick on. Not until I know what to do. I know that once I leave the apartment where I grew up, I will probably never return, and I am not ready to close the door. This place has seen so much pain and anguish. I want to fix it all, make it all right, but I can't. I don't have my mother to guide me, to help me understand all this new information.

I have this gift my mother left me; a new door to walk through when I am ready. I am not ready yet. It is all too overwhelming and it is too soon. I need family, friends, and space; anything to save me from all the pain I am feeling. But most of all I need time.

I begin to think maybe I am not sure I even want to change my feelings. That will leave me so vulnerable, and I have built up so many walls. I begin to think maybe I am better off leaving things alone. It is safer that way. I won't have to open myself up to deeper pain. I won't have to face my ignorance. It would be so much easier to walk out the front door of this apartment and never look back. Just move on, close the door, I think. But I can never go back to the way things were. I have to move forward, just not quite yet.

I sit for a long time on the couch in my old bedroom, lost in my own thoughts. Once I walk out of this room I will be leaving my childhood behind forever.

My watch says 4:00 p.m. It is beginning to get dark outside. I need to go home. I just can't move from this couch. I finally get up, gather the papers, photographs, and documents, and put them into a shopping bag that my mother had saved. I pack up the few precious possessions of my family that I want to preserve, take the suitcase from my parents' bedroom, and head down the hall. I walk slowly toward the front door, each step giving me a new sense of purpose. I open the front door, step into the hall, and slam the door behind me. I have done it. I have faced my greatest fears and survived.

CHAPTER 10

Eva's Condolences

Three and a half long, excruciating months have gone by since the night I walked out of Columbia Presbyterian Hospital and saw my mother for the last time. I have not shared how my mother died with her contemporaries. I did not want them to look differently upon her, but I have told some of my friends and some family members. I need their support to survive myself.

I check my watch. It is 4:30 p.m. The mail lady usually pulls up to my house about now. Should I go out and check? I wonder. Maybe give her a couple more minutes. I'm not eager to see what she brings today.

There have been months of condolence cards, loving letters professing deep sympathy for my family. There have been packages of food and books on the subject of suicide and loss. It has all been overwhelming.

The mail has been steadily coming every day like clockwork. Just as the day begins to fade and the sky turns blood red, the mail truck comes into view as a reminder that I will have to face another stack of letters and cards. Each day I sit by my kitchen table looking out on the dull, gray landscape of winter as the day fades into blackness of night. I try my best to write a couple of kind words to thank each sender individually. Mostly I just sign the form thank you notes from the funeral home: "Thank you for your kindness, gratefully the

Rauch Family." Only in the last couple of weeks has the steady stream of condolence mail slowed down to a trickle.

It is 5:00 p.m. The mail must be in my mailbox by now. I walk down the driveway as I do every day at this time, expecting to get the usual junk mail and assortment of bills. As I reach for the mail inside the box, a small envelope catches my eye. I think, not another condolence card. I can't read one more compassionate message. Each note, although well meaning, has picked at this sore that will not heal.

Walking back up the driveway I debate whether to open this last card or simply toss it away. It could have gotten lost in the mail. I hold it in my hand and stare at the return address, which is unfamiliar.

I suppose it is my curiosity that has me open this last expression of sympathy. The note simply reads:

Dear Evelyn,
I knew your parents and your grandmother. I wish to express my deepest sympathy for the loss of your dear mother. I apologize for the lateness of this note but I just found out about your dear mother. Your grandmother was one of two people I admired most in my life. One was your grandmother and the other was Eleanor Roosevelt.
Fondly, Eva Neisser

Who is this person that I have never met? How does she know me? Neither my mother nor my grandmother had ever spoken of Eva. How did she know my family? Why was my grandmother so admired by her? I have so many questions. I keep staring at the note and the return address. What was Eva's connection to my family? Neisser sounds German. Maybe they knew each other in Germany?

My husband comes home at 6:30 p.m., and I am anxious to share this mystery with him. I hand him the small handwritten note.

"Who is Eva Neisser?" he asks.

"I have no idea," I answer.

"Well, you need to find out. She obviously knew your family very well."

My alarm clock reads midnight and I am lying in bed unable to sleep. My thoughts are still racing, trying to figure out who Eva is. Is she my mother's age and is she even German? In the timeline of my mother's life, where does she fit?

The suspense is maddening. I lie awake for hours wondering if I should try to find her number and call her or write to her. By morning I decide to write to her. Calling would be too forward. In the early morning sunlight I begin to write a short friendly response on one of the condolence thank you notes:

Dear Eva,
I was touched by your note of sympathy to me. I am not sure what your connection is to my family. I would like very much to talk to you. My phone number is 554-9094. Please feel free to call me at any time. I hope to hear from you soon.
Fondly, Evelyn Rauch

I put the note on the kitchen table and prepare breakfast. A part of me is eager for more information about my mother. There is another side that trembles with the idea that there may be much I don't know and possibly shouldn't know. What if Eva tells me things that will cause me more pain? How will I cope? What will I do with the information she might have? I decide I am not hungry for breakfast anymore.

As I walk back to the mailbox to send the note to Eva, the sun is shining brightly. The ground has a warm glow as if light is emanating from it. I reach for the handle of the mailbox to place the note to Eva in the box for the mailman to pick up. The metal is warm from the sun. I have a feeling of unsettling anticipation. What will Eva reply, or will there even be a response?

CHAPTER 11

The Answer

Three days have passed since I mailed the letter to Eva. All weekend I have not let the thought of Eva leave me. I am scared to learn more about my mother and my grandmother, and yet I desperately want to know more.

It is Monday morning. I wonder when or if she will call. The phone rings almost on cue as my thoughts have traveled in Eva's direction. I pick up the receiver and a voice in a familiar German accent says, "Is this the Rauch residence? Am I speaking to Evelyn Rauch?"

"I am Evelyn Rauch," I respond.

"This is Eva Neisser. I got your note, and it would be lovely if we could meet each other. Your grandmother and mother were dear friends of mine."

I have so many questions that I want to ask. I'd want to talk for an hour, but I realize that this would become an interrogation over the phone, so I simply say back, "That would be lovely."

"I am an old woman and I don't take long trips anymore. I wonder if you would be able to come to Vineland in New Jersey to see me. I hope that would not be too much trouble for you. I would be happy to invite you for lunch. Please bring your dear husband. It would be lovely to meet him, too," Eva says.

"Oh, it's no trouble at all. That would be wonderful," I say, not realizing where Vineland is in relation to where I live. We arrange to meet at her house for lunch in two weeks.

"I am so grateful for this opportunity to meet you. Thank you for your invitation for lunch. I look forward to Sunday," I say. "I will call again to confirm before we come."

"I will send you directions. Do you have a computer?" Eva asks.

"Yes, of course you can e-mail them to me. Thank you," I respond.

"Lovely!" Eva sings out. "See you on Sunday in two weeks."

I am amazed that this old lady has computer skills. My mother would never have touched a computer. But my grandmother would have learned how to use one. She was such a bright businesswoman. I was beginning to get a sense that my grandmother and Eva might have had a lot in common. I realized why the voice on the phone sounded so familiar—it could have been my grandmother's voice.

It has been a long time since I have heard my grandmother's voice. She has been dead for many years, but I will always remember her formidable presence. Omi, as I called her, was not your typical grandmother. She was always very patient with me, but she was more of a teacher than a grandmother. She would spend many hours playing Scrabble with me and reading to me. When I was old enough I would visit her at her place of business on Hudson Street in downtown Manhattan. To my young eyes she had the biggest desk in the world. Everyone called her Mrs. Lippmann, never Kathe. My grandmother had been the controller for one of the largest food importing businesses in the United States.

I would look forward to my visits to Hudson Street. My grandmother would have a plate of cookies imported from some exotic place for me to try. On the shelves of the showroom were all sorts of strange delicacies, fried beetles and freeze dried grasshoppers to name a few. There were crystallized candied flowers from France and chocolate covered ants from the Far East. On the walls were also posters of faraway places featuring specialty foods from the country of their origin. I would fantasize about traveling to these countries with my grandmother. Omi would play a game with me: she showed me the food that the company she worked for imported and I would have to guess where it came from. Grandma made a lesson out of everything.

Everyone knew my grandmother and showered her with affection. She had the right combination of toughness, humility, common sense, and good intensions. Her voice always commanded attention and compliance. I respected her and obeyed her, as did everyone. My mother loved her mother deeply, but she was never able to stand up to her. My grandmother's will was too strong. When she wanted something done there was no one who would stop her; and she always had the last word. But she spoke in such a polite manner that it was impossible to oppose her. She was the most formidable force in our family and had the final say in family discussions. Kathe must have been a powerful figure in Eva's life as well. It is becoming clear that it was possible that my grandmother could have had a profound effect on anyone's life given the right circumstances.

It had been a long time since I thought so much about Omi. It is only me who is left. I have such a limited knowledge of my mother's and grandmother's past. There are so many gaps. I need to fill in the blanks. Eva may be the key to unlock many closed doors. The phone rings again and my thoughts are interrupted. It would be days till my mind would revisit the mystery of Eva Neisser.

CHAPTER 12

The Trip to Vineland

It is Friday afternoon and the phone rings. It is Eva Neisser calling to confirm our Sunday date. I am slightly embarrassed by the fact that she is calling me to confirm as I had offered to do this. But I realize this is good old German efficiency. "Always cross your t's and dot your i's," my grandmother would say.

"Did you get my directions? Do you have any questions, and do you have any dietary restrictions?" Eva asks.

"I received the directions, they are very clear, and I eat almost anything. Please don't go to any trouble," I answer.

"Lovely, then I will look forward to you and your dear husband's visit. See you for lunch at twelve thirty," Eva says.

"I will look forward to meeting you, too," I say and put down the receiver.

I decide that I should bring a tape recorder to our meeting. Saturday is a busy day putting together my mother's papers and preparing for our visit. I don't even know if I should bring these things to our first meeting. I am hungry for answers to my mother's past, and almost desperate to have a better understanding of what led my mother to this bitter end. I am hoping that in some way it will also absolve me of responsibility.

Surely Eva has no idea of how important this visit is to me. I hope she will not be put off by all the questions I will have for her. She

65

thinks this is just a friendly visit. I have to remember not to come on too strong or open wounds that have scarred over the years. I will have to watch my words and ease into a discussion of my family's past. Let Eva run the conversation. I am thinking too much. I'm scared, sad, and excited to meet Eva. My emotions are all over the place. Thank goodness David is coming with me—he will help me to calm down.

It is Sunday morning. David and I go over the directions and realize that it will take about two hours to reach Vineland, New Jersey. So we start out on our journey at 10:00 a.m., leaving us extra time in case we make any wrong turns. The ride to Vineland is long and monotonous. How rural the southern part of the state is. There are miles and miles of nothing. Some areas don't even have any greenery. Why would anyone every want to live here?

"There has to be a story as to why Eva moved to Vineland. I can't imagine it was because she loved the area," I snicker.

David and I have a good laugh. I haven't laughed in a long time. Eva's directions are impeccable. We have not made one wrong turn yet, but the ride is beginning to get to me and I feel impatient and jumpy. I keep looking at my watch hoping that this long ride will end soon. Finally, there is a sign ahead that reads, "Welcome to Vineland, New Jersey." We are now on Landis Boulevard riding through a town that has seen better days. The neighborhood looks as if it has not progressed past the late 1940s; as if it had been caught in a time warp. We arrive at a modest garden apartment complex. Again I wonder how Eva ended up in this place.

Outside the doorway to the garden apartment stands a rather stout woman who appears to be slightly older than my mother. This must be Eva.

"Hi. How lovely to meet you. Please follow me. How was your ride?" she asks.

"Oh it was fine, we are thrilled to meet you finally," I answer. "I hope all of this is not too much trouble for you."

"Nonsense. I am delighted you could come," Eva answers, "and this must be your dear husband, David?"

We follow Eva down a narrow hallway to her first floor apartment. It is modestly furnished, but I notice immediately that there are many old lithographs, drawings, and photographs hanging all over the walls of this apartment that seem to be from Europe. This further confirms my earlier suspicions that the relationship Eva had with my mother and grandmother was from the years they lived in Germany. But what had my grandmother accomplished that won her such admiration from Eva? I imagine that these are the questions I should start with today. I think that Eva will be more interested in speaking about her relationship with my family than looking through my documents. So this is where I will start and then see what happens.

CHAPTER 13

Lunch with Eva

Eva's apartment is small but comfortable. The dining room table is set with what looks like antique china. David and I have brought flowers and chocolate. I can tell that she is pleased with our gifts. She takes a vase and sets the eighteen pink roses on the table and puts the chocolate on a plate with a doily. Eva has gone out of her way to make a lovely lunch. Our conversation begins rather awkwardly with the usual formalities. How are my children? She has heard I have a boy and a girl. How is my job? What are my interests?

After we get past these pleasantries, I ask the question I have wanted to ask since I learned where Eva lived. "Eva, how did you come to live in Vineland?"

"My father was an immigrant from Germany. When the Nazis came to power we lost everything and we had to flee Germany. When we arrived in the United States we had no means of support. My father started a small importing business with his brother-in-law. Our offices were in downtown Manhattan on Hudson Street and Chambers Street. His uncle, who immigrated several years earlier, had a connection to a former law clerk who married into a very wealthy family that owned Rokeach Kosher Soups. They agreed to allow my father and his brother to sell their soups. At the time, more well-off Jewish families were classified as affidavit givers for the Jewish refugees who immigrated. These families were afraid that they would have to support these refugees, so they were only too happy to let them sell Rokeach soups and other delicatessen items from door-to-door. They became Berwin Trading and Importing Company's sales force. I became their translator and took care of all the correspondence in English because I had taken English in school and was quite gifted in language studies. About this time your grandmother came to work for my father and his brother as the bookkeeper for the business."

So this is the connection of Eva to my grandmother. But how did she get this job and why? I have so many questions, but I do not want to interrupt her story.

Eva continues, "Goodman's Matzo and Noodles was owned by one of my father's close friends and many refugees made items like pickled red cabbage, pickles, and sweet syrups. The business took off because items like these were new to the United States and a lot of Jewish families clamored for them. My father and his brother imported many items from Europe and Israel. But as World War II took shape, many of the ships that carried these imported items came under fire and were sunk. Berwin Importing and Trading Company could not fill its orders. We used to joke about how the salespeople all made money but we didn't. They would get paid for their orders, but we couldn't fill them. The business eventually went under. It was bought out by a Mr. Wolf and a Mr. Lowenstein. The business then became Liberty Import and then Century Foods, one of the largest importing businesses in the United States Your grandmother stayed with the firm until she was well into her 80s. She was one of the most intelligent persons I have ever met.

"My father's spirit was broken but he needed to support his family. The Jewish Agricultural Society purchased large tracks of land in southern New Jersey during the turn of the century to provide for the Russian refugees who were fleeing the pogroms in Russia during that time. They leased land to immigrants in Vineland for very little money to help those fleeing the Nazis to work and be self-sufficient; not to be a burden on the US government.

"Vineland was the center of the US poultry business. One day my father came home and told us we were moving to Vineland, New Jersey. He had bought a chicken farm. And so my father became a chicken farmer. Max Berwin never made much money from the poultry business. He had lost his enthusiasm. I suppose that was from losing the importing business and his successful business in Germany, but he was able to provide for us. We were very poor but happy to be alive. I met my husband here and started a small travel agency in town. Time passed and I just never left, even though the town has deteriorated a lot. Vineland has been my home for more than sixty years."

So now it is confirmed. Eva grew up in Germany and she must have known my family from those days. So it is time to ask the burning question: "Eva, how do you know my family? I was so touched by your expression of sympathy, but I have never heard your name mentioned by my mother or my grandmother, so I have no idea how you came to know them or have such high regard for my grandmother."

I can tell that Eva is a bit put off by the fact that I have no idea who she is. I hope I have not done something wrong by telling her this. It will be terrible if I spoil this connection to my past.

Eva begins by saying that she is surprised that neither Steffi nor Kathe had mentioned her over the years, but that my mother and grandmother probably did not want to bring up the past.

"I knew your dear mother and wonderful grandmother all my life. Your grandmother, Kathe, and your grandfather, Ernest, were dear friends of my parents in Breslau, Germany, where we all grew up. The photos, lithographs, and drawings on the walls are those of our town. Ernest and Kathe Lippmann and my parents were the best of friends.

"My father and your grandfather were part of a small musical group called the Musikalisch-Literarischer-Verein. Altogether there were seven men in this group of talented musicians. These men were very successful business owners, but their true passion was music. Your grandfather was the youngest in the group by several years, but because of his great operatic voice he was accepted quite readily. Your grandmother was an accomplished pianist and accompanied these talented fellows.

"They practiced all week after work. On Saturday evenings they would get together with their families. Each week another member of the group would host the event at his house, cook a wonderful meal, and the musical group would perform after dinner. Some of the members where Orthodox Jews and therefore could not perform before sundown, and so we would start the music after sundown about eight thirty. The whole week our families would prepare for and look forward to the end of the week. Our housekeepers would create special meals and try out new recipes.

"Our homes were always filled with music and laughter. Your grandmother would play the piano and your mother would sit on top of it and sing along with her father as they practiced. They were such a wonderful and happy family in those days. Even your dear mother already showed talent in her singing abilities at such a young age. She was really just a little child at that time."

"So you and my mother were playmates growing up?" I interrupt.

"No, not exactly," Eva continues. "My sister and I were several years older than Steffi. Our families were so close, and so we were thrown together every week at these family evenings, holidays, and birthdays. Your mother was young and sometimes she would get cranky and misbehave. Your grandfather, Ernest, would always say, "Children are to be seen but not heard." Your grandmother would scold Steffi: "Why can't you behave like those well-mannered Berwin girls?" We would smile and nod, which of course made matters much worse. So we tolerated each other in those days. We had no choice in the matter; but I would not have called us playmates.

"These wonderful years were very short lived. Your grandfather died very suddenly from an infection after a hernia operation. Your mother was only seven-years-old at the time. Your grandmother went into a deep depression. She had waited several long years during World War I when your grandfather went off to fight for Germany, to marry Ernest. He returned defeated, which took its toll for some time and in just eight short years he was gone. From what I can recall, the Saturday musical evenings stopped after that.

"Since your mother and I had only seen each other at the family dinners and events, we really did not have much contact with each other in our early childhood after that. But our parents stayed close. Your grandmother had the responsibility of taking care of herself, her daughter, and her mother and mother-in-law. Since your grandfather died so young, he had not accumulated any money and there were no men in the family to support these women. Your grandmother had no choice but to rise to the occasion and take on the responsibility of supporting the family.

"It was decided by family friends, including my father, to help Kathe rescue her husband's failing insurance business. They would help her by taking insurance policies out on their lives. These men all had extensive business assets. This helped Kathe get started, and with her fierce determination, despite the deteriorating political climate in Germany, she became quite successful. She did what needed to be done, as she would always say.

"She was one of the most capable people I have ever known. You must understand that in those days woman did not work. It was virtually unheard of that a woman would own her own business. But Kathe was tough and could hold her own against any man. She took wonderful care of your mother, but Steffi had to be in the company of her grandmothers and the housekeeper much of the time. That had to be confusing for her and she must have missed your grandmother a lot. Also, the sudden loss of her father had to be devastating. Things changed so quickly and she was so young. Now, please help yourself to some cold cuts. Please eat."

I am so taken with the story that Eva is telling us that I have totally forgotten about eating. I haven't taken a bite yet. It is as if time has stopped and I have been transported back to Germany in the 1930s. I feel I am living every word that Eva is telling me.

"I promise I'll eat, but please go on," I beg.

"The situation in Germany was getting progressively worse with each passing year. Jewish children were being tormented in the public schools and anti-Semitism was on the rise. You could feel it in the air everywhere. But our parents were very skillful in protecting us and shielding us from most of the hurtful propaganda that was circulating at the time. It was decided by our parents that we would all go to private schools, that way we would not be subjected to any more harassment. Because your mother was younger and not quite as interested in her studies, we were sent to different schools. After that I only saw your mother at birthday parties of our parents' friends' children that we were forced to go to. In those days we were not the best of friends, but our parents developed a deep bond. Your grandmother relied on her friends for business advice and guidance. As the situation in Germany worsened, her relationships with these friends became more and more important, and Kathe's strength helped them to hold on through very tough times.

"The first inkling that the tide was turning in Germany came with Hitler's book *Mein Kampf*, in which he laid out his murderous aspirations for Germany. But our families and most Jews in Germany believed these were the ravings of a mad man. No one took it seriously and no one had any idea that what was contained in that book would ever come to fruition.

"In 1933 Hitler came to power and became prime minister of Germany. He established the first concentration camp, but only communists were interred at that time. By 1934 Hitler had declared himself both chancellor and president of Germany. That made him the absolute ruler with no opposition. The situation for Jews in Germany began to deteriorate very quickly from then on. Still my father and his friends believed this was just a passing phase in Germany history. They had survived hard times before, and they would do it again.

After all, they had fought in World War I and survived the aftermath of the war.

"In 1936 when the Nazis began to boycott Jewish businesses and Jews were no longer allowed to vote, your wise grandmother realized that conditions in Germany were only going to get worse. She began the process that would lead to her escape with Steffi from Germany. She tried to convince her friends that it was time to make plans to leave, but they all thought that was too extreme; our families still believed that conditions would change and the country would stop the insanity.

Kathe had a wealthy distant relative in the United States. Your grandmother always referred to him as Cousin Abe. She wrote to him and described the desperate situation that she and Steffi were in and asked if he would be willing to sign an affidavit to vouch for them so they could immigrate to America. I know this because I helped write that letter.

"At first Cousin Abe flatly turned Kathe down. But she applied anyway for a visa to travel to the United States to visit him, in Helena, Arkansas, and convince him to sponsor her and her daughter and sign the affidavit. Your courageous grandmother left her home and her family during those troubled times and traveled alone by steamship for two weeks across the Atlantic to the United States. She spoke only a little English at the time, but she could make herself understood.

"At first Cousin Abe was reluctant to even see your grandmother. But once he did he saw a true lady through and through; a fine, strong, independent woman who truly seemed desperate to save herself and her daughter. Not only did he agree to sign the affidavit, but he also sent money every month for years to help Kathe get on her feet again.

"So Kathe returned to Germany with the paper she hoped would save her and Steffi's lives. But there was very little rejoicing when she returned. She knew she could not take her mother or her mother-in-law with her. Cousin Abe had only agreed to sponsor her and her daughter. Besides, the fact was that your great-grandmothers were too old and too frail to make such a trip. From then on it was a waiting game till your grandmother's quota number came up; a waiting game against time. Would her number come up before she was dragged away to a concentration camp or worse?"

That ticking clock again. How it had affected all our lives. It is 2:30 p.m. David and I had only planned to stay till 3:00 p.m. to avoid the rush hour traffic; but I can't leave now. "Please go on," I urge.

"Your grandmother was worried that their quota number would not come up in time or that other terrible events might prevent them from ever getting out of Germany, so she began to work on the possibility of sending Steffi to England on the *Kindertransport*. The *Kindertransport* was a rescue mission to save Jewish children from the Nazis by sending them chaperoned to safety in the United Kingdom where they would be sheltered by English families. But Steffi was seventeen-years-old and the cut off for this was sixteen, so other arrangements had to be made. I think that she went to some sort of school for domestic servants in preparation for a job as a domestic in England, but I can't be sure."

"Eva," I interrupt, "if you don't mind, I think I have a document referring to just this subject. A paper I found among my mother's things. Can I take a moment to look for it? I would love to show it to you. Maybe it will jog your memory."

I shuffle through the papers I brought with us and locate the one in question. It reads:

With reference to your advertisement in the Times I wish to inform you that my daughter would be very grateful to get the announced post in your family. My daughter is a girl of seventeen years, very strong and healthy and very educated. After terminating high school, she was working as a probationer in a home for girls and has learned many duties to take care of a household. Then she was trained in a course for gymnastic and medical massage. My daughter intended to go to the United States and her waiting number will be called in the fall of 1939; therefore, she would be very glad to

get the possibility of living, during the meantime, in England. It is only possible to enter England by getting a permit through the home office. I beg you instantly to help us in these troubles, and to do the necessary applications. Enclosed you will find some photos. The references you asked for are:
Mrs. D.D. Braham
904 Collingwood
Dolphin Square
London S W 1, Tel. Victoria 3800
Mrs. M. Juliusburger
41 Southfields
Hendon
N.W. 4
I hope to hear from you as soon as possible and remain
Yours Faithfully

I explain, "This must have been a copy of a letter of inquiry that was sent to someone in England. There is also another paper."

Charlotte Hulsen I hereby confirm that Miss Steffi Lippmann, Breslau, has made a six weeks course in baking and cookery with me. I have the impression that she is perfect in cooking and baking now.
She was always very eager and willing to help me at the work. By the level of her skill, she knew very well how to dispose best of her time for cooking.
Breslau, August 15th 1937
signed: Charlotte Hulsen
Kochschile Charlotte Hulsen

Eva continues, "So you see your grandmother was desperate to get Steffi out of Germany as soon as possible. I remember how desperate we all were at that time. Your grandmother had seen the handwriting on the wall much sooner than my family, and yet it was still a race against time for her as well. On the night of November 9, 1938—Kristallnacht—hundreds of synagogues were smashed to pieces and burned in one night of horrific violence against Jews. Jewish businesses and shops were destroyed. I think your mother was still in Germany to see this terrible display of anti-Semitism. The Holocaust had begun. I remember the day your mother left for England, although I don't remember the exact date. It was so frightening and sad. Your mother and your grandmother only had each other, and now they would have to part ways and go it alone. I am sure your grandmother was terrified that she would never see Steffi again, but she did not show it. She reassured her daughter that soon they would be together again and to be strong. In a sense she was reassuring herself as well. She hugged Steffi and kissed her good-bye.

"Soon after that my father was thrown in jail. My father had a very large and reputable business in Germany. The Nazis had wanted my father to sign over his business to them, and when he refused, they dragged him off to jail. We lost everything. The Nazis took our bank accounts, our business, and every bit of our money. In order to get my father out of jail and leave the country we needed cash immediately and that is when your grandmother actually saved our lives at great risk to her own.

"You remember I told you that when your grandfather died his friends took out large life insurance policies to jump start Kathe's business? Well, your grandmother cashed in my father's policy as if he was dead. We got 30,000 marks. To us it was a fortune. That money went to bribe the officials to get my father out of jail and to buy us our freedom. It took 25,000 marks to buy my family a certificate for Palestine and the rest went for shipboard passage. Your grandmother simply said, "One good turn deserves another." I owe my very existence to your courageous and loving grandmother. I imagine that she may have helped some of the other families in our group of friends in the same way. I don't know. She never again spoke about this, but all the others survived as well so it is conceivable.

"It is impossible for you to realize what kind of risk she took. She had already secured an immigration number for herself and Steffi.

If the Nazis had caught on to her deception she most surely would have been sent to the gas chamber and Steffi may never have made it to the United States. She is my hero. We escaped to Palestine and then made our way to the United States. Your grandmother stayed in Germany to wait for her immigration number to come up.

"Imagine what a frightening time that had to have been for her. She told us later that as she prepared for her exodus from Germany, she put all her belongs in a container that was sent by ship to Norway. She sewed all her jewelry into the featherbeds hoping to hide it that way. All her furnishings, every precious thing she had, went into that container. It was widely speculated that Norway would not be attacked by the Germans and her belongings would be safe in the harbor until she would either return to Europe or send for them. But that turned out to be a falsehood. Norway's harbor was attacked and all her belongings were lost. She was left with nothing. Your grandmother was never bitter about that. She was happy to be alive. From what I can recall she never complained about anything. She was such an optimistic and strong person."

Now I understand why my grandmother never wanted material things for herself. She lived a plain life and she was frugal, but she was quite extravagant when it came to my mother. Every birthday all the gifts that my grandmother gave Steffi would be displayed for all to see. I never understood that. But now it is clear that she wanted to shower my mother with things, and make up for all the possessions that had been destroyed. She wanted my father and his family to see that my mother had fine things and that she could provide them. I always thought it was to spite my father somehow, but now I see it for what it actually was. She wanted Steffi to have what she had lost.

Unfortunately, those displays caused a great deal of tension in my home. My father was always resentful of the extravagant gifts from his mother-in-law. He felt that it was his place to provide for my mother, and when he didn't have the money for those items my grandmother would step in and provide them. He never understood, nor did I, that it was Kathe's guilt that drove her.

My mother's childhood had been filled with pitfalls. From birth there had been hurdles to overcome. Not long before she died, my grandmother explained the circumstances surrounding my mother's birth: "I became pregnant with Steffi soon after your grandfather had just returned from the war. He had been away for so long, and I did not want a baby to enter the picture of our lives at that time. I was very depressed, but finally consoled myself by thinking I was carrying a baby boy and would be giving your grandfather a son. When I gave birth to your mother, I was inconsolable and refused to even see her. Several months went by before I finally realized what I was doing to our infant daughter. Steffi was being cared for by our housekeeper and nanny, Franciona. One day Franciona got sick and could not care for Steffi. I had no choice but to step in. Once I held your mother in my arms I wept for what I had done. I never forgave myself, but I have spent my life trying to make up for it."

So much is clearer to me now; it all fits together. My grandmother was always trying to control what she had no control over: my mother's ultimate happiness. In the end, we all failed Steffi.

But what about Steffi and Kathe's move to the United States and their reunion there? The hour is getting late. It is 4:00 p.m. and I promised David we would be on the road by 3:00 p.m.. to avoid too much traffic. The rest of the story would have to wait till Eva and I got together again.

As we get ready to leave, I remember the papers that I have brought with me. "Eva," I begin, "do you think you might have time to translate some of these letters I have with me? They are from my mother to my grandmother and they are dated. I have not been able to decipher them. I can understand spoken German pretty well, but I can't read a line of it. Maybe we could discuss them on another visit if that would not be too much trouble?"

"Leave them with me," she says. "I will try my best to translate them for you."

"We will meet again soon I hope. Thank you so much again for the lunch and your graciousness. Please let me know what you learn from these letters. I will anxiously await your translations," I answer.

"Evelyn, I am an old lady and it may take me some time, but I will try to get to it soon," Eva replies in a somewhat impatient tone.

I hope I haven't offended her in some way or asked too much of her too quickly. Her defensive tone is upsetting and I fear I may lose this valuable woman's help and friendship.

"Eva, if it is too much, please, it's all right I can have someone else translate them for me."

"I am fine with it. I just need some time to do it. Things go rather slowly for me these days, but I will get to it. I promise."

Eva's words are reassuring and I feel somewhat calmer with my decision to bring the papers up at this visit. By now I should know that German Jews on the whole don't tolerate being taken advantage of. They are defensive and tough. Life has made them that way. Their very survival depended on these traits. My mother and grandmother were the same way. I always thought my mother, in particular, had a strong persecution complex. She seemed to keep a mental list of all the wrong that had been dealt her way over her lifetime. She couldn't let go of the past even though she couldn't confront it either. I am beginning to understand why. The Germans had tried to take away all sense of self-esteem and pride the Jews had, and because they always considered themselves Germans first, this struck at the very core of German Jewry. The only way they had to confront this systematic attack on their character was to become adaptable, defensive, and tough. And yet those who lived through the Holocaust had done the impossible. They had survived unspeakable horrors and become successful, useful members of American society.

I think my grandmother fared better than my mother because she was an adult when her life came crashing down around her. My mother lacked the mental tools to cope as well because she was just a child when Hitler came to power. But she must have been very strong in those days to have survived the many months in England alone without her mother. I can't wait to hear what my mother's letters say. But I will have to contain myself until Eva translates them for me.

The ride home is long and monotonous. Southern New Jersey's landscape is flat, with lower middle-class row houses lining the main roads. The sky is darkening and rain is beginning to fall. I am glad that we visited Eva, but I also have a deep burning in the pit of my stomach, much like the sickening feeling I had when I answered the phone so many months ago and a stranger told me, "You better come to your mother's apartment quickly. I think your mother is in deep trouble. There are notes." What will the letters I left with Eva say? Will they help me in some way? Is this all just continuing the pain that is already too much to bear? The voices in my head are loud and angry. Why didn't somebody tell me? Why do I have to find things out this way? Why didn't my mother trust me to understand? David and I are silent most of the way home. I am grateful for Eva's help and friendship, but at the same time I wish I didn't need to know. But I do.

CHAPTER 14

Looking through Steffi's Papers

It is Monday morning and I am sitting in the kitchen thinking about my visit with Eva yesterday. I decide to go through the box containing my mother's papers once again. Maybe there is a letter or a document I forgot to look at and show Eva. Inside the box are wonderful pictures of better times when my parents were first married. The photos are in black and white. There are pictures of my parents' friends on vacation and skiing. My mother actually has a smile on her face and seems so happy.

The photos speak to me. I see a different Steffi: a young, vibrant woman, happy and free. There are pictures of my grandmother when she was young, and photos of my grandfather. I see Steffi's resemblance to my grandfather in the old photographs of my mother.

I remember that Eva told me about my grandfather's operatic voice, and how my mother inherited his musical talent. I understand now why music was always so important in my home. Steffi must have heard her father's voice in every aria that she listened to. I am sure it was a great disappointment to her that I did not share her love for music. Only now as I get older has my appreciation for classical music developed. I will listen with a new ear from now on. I hope I too will hear my mother's and my grandfather's voices in the music I have yet to listen to.

This is my heritage and my children's heritage. These documents and photographs are their ancestor's legacy. I must take care of them, not just throw them in a box like yesterday's junk mail. But what, in the end, will I do with all of this stuff? What will it mean to my children if I, myself, don't understand all these papers? I imagine with time it will come to me. For now I need to decipher what I can.

There are cookbooks that are in longhand, written and signed by Franciona Schmidt, my mother's German nanny and housekeeper. I will want to get these translated, too. Maybe my mother's best friend, Ilsa, will be able to help me with this. It is so frustrating not being able to read the German myself. I spent my childhood hearing more German spoken than English, but I never learned how to read German. Who would have thought that it would be so important?

I make copies of the cookbooks, not wanting to send the precious originals, and write a note to Ilsa explaining how I found these among my mother's papers and would she be so kind as to help me translate them.

Ilsa is two years younger than my mother. Her father is the man that sent the twenty-four red roses every year to my mother. I don't think she ever knew about her father's relationship with my mother. Ilsa is the only one out of my mother's friends that I have told about my mother's suicide. Everyone else thinks she died of pneumonia.

I call California to tell her that I am sending these copies to her and would appreciate her help.

"Evie, of course I will help you as best I can. I will call you when the copies arrive and we'll see what we can piece together. How are you doing? I love you and so did your dear mother. I know she didn't mean to hurt you. She must have been out of her mind and in great pain to do something like that," Ilsa replies. "She went through so much to have you. You know she had a miscarriage before you were born. I suppose having a child was both happy and frightening for her. Happy, because she finally had someone of her very own to love, and frightening because she was afraid to lose you once again."

Ilsa is right: my mother was always fearful of where I was or what I was doing that she couldn't control. As time went on and I began to develop my own mind, that obsession worsened. I spent more and more time with friends and less and less time at home. That only made my mother more anxious and possessive of my time. I realize now that I was all she had, but in that lies the true problem between us. I was the one possession she could not let go of and I wanted to have my own life.

"I know she didn't mean to hurt me, but it still hurts anyway," I answer. "I know you knew her best, so I appreciate your help and comfort. Thank you, Ilsa, we will speak soon," I say and then hang up. I begin to cry. I haven't cried in two days. That's the longest stretch I've had since my mother passed away.

In typically efficient German style, the translations of the cookbooks arrive just ten days later with a note attached.

Dear Evie,
My ninety-three-year-old friend tried to translate these books, but was of no help. I even asked a friend of mine in Fort Lee, New Jersey who visits old people in a nursing home nearby, but that didn't work either.
I hope the enclosed is some help. Many of the recipes are duplicates, and there are many different handwritings. Whatever I did translate was done with love.
Ilsa

As I read through the translations, I can see that most of the recipes are desserts. How odd that in those troubled times these would be the recipes that would be smuggled out of Germany.

Some of them seem familiar—I have tasted these sweets over the years. My mother must have adopted these confections into her American cookery. I pick up the phone to thank Ilsa for her quick response.

"Evie," she says, "you know your grandfather died when your mother was very young. Your grandmother had to go to work and

Steffi was left alone with the housekeeper most of the day. Franciona was a lovely person as far as I remember. I was so young at the time, but I know Steffi loved to cook all her life. She got her first lessons in Franciona's kitchen. The Lippmanns were no lightweights as you know, so desserts were very important in the Lippmann household. I imagine that is why there are so many dessert recipes. For years during your mother's adolescence, the whole week was spent preparing for the Saturday night performance of the Musikalisch-Literarischer-Verein. Your mother must have spent a great deal of time in the kitchen."

So that is why my mother loved to cook and my grandmother could hardly boil water. Steffi was taught by the best, and Kathe had no time for such domestic matters. She was too busy supporting the family. My mother truly grew up to be an excellent cook, but ironically her desserts were never her strong point. I guess in this way she had forged her own path.

My mother & grandmother ....

My Mother.....

Kathe and Ernest's Wedding
1920

Steffi and Eugene'
wedding 194

Evelyn and David's Wedding
1970

Grandfather Ernest

Ernest and his mother

Kathe's Mother

The Lioppman Family

Grandmother Kathe

Eva Neisser

Steffi and Kathe

Grandmother Kathe &
Evelyn 1965

Breslau, Germany

Town Square

Memorial to Members
of the Temple

Synagogue

CHAPTER 15

Steffi's Letters

There is a large, thick, brown envelope in my mail box. I can hardly restrain myself from opening it as I walk quickly back to the house carrying the day's assortment of mail. Eva has kept her promise. Once inside the house, I take a deep breath and quickly rip open the envelope. There are two letters and a poem. The earliest one from January 20, 1939 reads:

My most beloved, golden mother!
It is already 10:30 at night, but I still want to start to write to you. It gets late almost every evening, and it is terrible that I neglect my writing, but I am usually too tired. After I waited for a long time for mail from you, I finally received your letter dated December 24. I mailed a letter before yesterday, which I stupidly left lying around for a few days. I will send this letter via air mail, but even that takes so long. Thank you very much for the affidavit that you sent me. I am of course already very impatient and nervous because I don't hear anything, I don't know what I should be doing from here. I could, of course, go to the consulate, but that is really quite difficult. The consulate is only open in the morning, and it is hard for me to leave here at that time. However, I could arrange that. I would not learn very much. In any case, I will wait until the end of the month. Yesterday I was at the Loewes who also think that there is nothing else that I can do. They have not heard anything either. It has been said that their number should appear in February. I wish

I would be ready to travel at that time, also. It would be wonderful if we could travel together. I cannot do anything about transportation before I am asked to appear at the consulate. In any case, the route through Italy will be impossible because, as I already wrote to you, I will not be able to get a transit visa. Nobody gets that. But I would hope to have that worry already. Otherwise I am well. I like the work here. There is a really nice relationship between the guests and the employees and also between the employees and especially Dr. and Mrs. Pick; one of the owners who works in the kitchen is very nice. I think I already wrote you that I work mornings in the rooms. I clean four rooms, two bathrooms, and the staircase. Early in the morning I bring the breakfast trays to the rooms. I have to finish at 1:00 p.m. Then I help serve. After the guests have eaten, the German employees eat together. Afterward everyone is really supposed to be off for one and a half hours, but often that does not happen depending on what there is to do. In the afternoon I usually help to set the table for dinner. Then I have to open the beds in the bedrooms. At 7:15 is dinner where I serve again. Dinner lasts until about 8:30 p.m. Then we help with the enormous dish washing, and then tables have to be set for breakfast. This is a very large enterprise. There are two large buildings. Meals are served in the one that houses the kitchen. There are about forty guests without employees and the family of the owners. They are starting to occupy a third house already. This is one of the few boarding houses that is fully occupied. I have to speak English, but it is a real advantage to be with people who are in a similar situation. Everybody is very nice to me, especially Mrs. Pick who is a lovely lady. The only bad thing is Gerda Voremberg who has constant arguments with Aunt Lene and who is extremely unkind to me. The reason is that she is jealous of me. She is on miserable terms with Aunt Lene right now, but they've become best friends again, crazy. They are both difficult people. Most likely she will leave within the next two weeks. It is certainly not easy to get along with Aunt Lene, and if I would not agree with everything she says, we would also have constant arguments. However, she is kind and means well. She sews and mends everything for me, does my laundry because I would hardly have time to do any of this. I learned to accept things and am sure that I will not yell anymore. You write that you are afraid that I will not write truthfully anymore. Actually, I have always told you everything truthfully and have never let you doubt that I was not particularly happy at Northwood. Yes, those months were really not easy, but it could have been worse. That you want to send money is totally unnecessary, because the money that we had to pay at the house of Frida Gllicksmann. I of course took from the money that you had sent me some time ago. I still have 12 P from that. Therefore, you really don't have to send me anything. Aunt Lene also already saved 15 P. You will only have to send something for the ticket for the boat. The Bloomsburg house does not give any fare contribution at the present time. If it only would happen already. And how are you, my darling, are you working hard? I can't wait to hear if you are still at Berwin's. Are you really totally well? I already worried because I had no news for such a long time. Please be careful. Oh, one really has to bear a lot. Yesterday I went to the movies with a young girl who also works here. We saw "Professor Mamlock." I don't know if you ever heard of it. The film shows the conditions in Germany under the present regime and how the Jews are treated, etc. It was horrible. The young girl was terribly upset since both her parents are still in Germany. Then I am always relieved. Tomorrow is my day off. I am planning to go to Renatel and then to Loewe. Recently I wrote to grandma and Aunt Kathe. My behavior to everybody is very bad now. I have not seen Goldber for an eternity. I should get in touch with Juiusburgers and the same with Lippmanns. All of them don't know where I am, but I really don't have any time. Once a week a free afternoon and evening and with the very great distances it is impossible to do very much. I am sorry, but I have to end because they want to go to sleep. So stay well, write soon, and be lovingly embraced by my longing for you. Steffi.

I always knew how close my grandmother and mother were to each other. But as I read the translation of this letter it is obvious why: they were two women who shared in a true life drama together. Both mother and daughter were so independent, and yet so dependent on each other for their emotional survival. There is a year span between this letter and the following letter. I can only imagine the fear and frustration that my mother and grandmother felt while Steffi waited for word that she would be able to finally leave England and be reunited with her mother. Each day must have felt like an eternity as the clock ticked on and days turned into months.

Eva writes at the top of the next letter: "This letter dated 27 January 1940 relates to your mother's booking passage from London to New York at a time when German U-boats sunk a great many ships, which actually sailed in large convoys. Your grandmother was an absolute wreck worrying about the choice between the "Blitz" bombing of London and the danger at sea, which was understandable."

January 27, 1940
My dearest, beloved, precious little Mummy,
When you receive this letter, you will probably be able to welcome me a few days later. When I think about it, that we shall see each other again in about three weeks, I could go crazy with joy over this great fortune. You will have received my telegram, and I can imagine how great the surprise and joy were. When I received the summons, on the morning of the twenty-fourth to come to the consulate on the twenty-sixth, I executed 1000 jumps into the air. On the twenty-sixth I then went, shaking and jittery, accompanied by Aunt Leuchen, and after waiting five hours, I walked out as the lucky owner of the visa. On the very same day I booked my passage on the Cunard Line after first talking at great length with many clever people. Dear Mummy, I had to commit this lie and leave you in the dark about my voyage. I know full well that you would not have permitted it at all, but believe me, you and all the others over there cannot judge the situation here, and what is right and wrong. We have forty-five guests here in the house, and of these every single one told me to travel by English convoy. The possibility to go via Genoa is simply not available. The mere mention of this proves that you (in the plural, meaning people of the United States) are not informed. I don't know on what ship I will travel, since I won't know it until I am on it myself. I also won't be able to send a telegram from the ship and hope that someone will do so for

me. Just in case, I am writing this letter today. I will sail in the beginning or middle of February. So when you receive this letter you will know that you can expect me on the next or second next ship of the Cunard Line. You will have to find out the exact information when it will arrive. So I hope you will forgive me for acting independently. I have saved you a lot of excitement by it, and saved years of both our lives by doing so. So, my beloved, I will end this letter. We shall soon be able to talk about everything in person. Oh, Mummy, I am so utterly happy in the thought to be with you soon. So here's to a healthy and happy reunion.
Ten thousand warm regards and kisses from your unspeakably happy,
Steffi

Eva wrote at the bottom of her translation: "Note that in January of 1940 your mother was probably eighteen-years-old or younger, and had to make a decision to risk her life on the crossing or amid falling bombs. She protected her mother from worrying until she was almost to America by sending the letter and not sending a telegram with her intentions. This was the kind of situation we who grew up at that time were faced with: parents in Gestapo jails, selling or giving away one's possessions, torn from a secure and protected life, thrown into hard labor, poverty, and danger. Scratch anyone of our generation and you get a similar story. That does not detract from the courage and admirable qualities of your dear mother. It just goes to show how brave she was and how she managed with sudden maturity and compassion. Our children should know this and compare it to their own cushioned lives, and be proud of their family! PS: We were there when this letter arrived and waited anxiously with your grandmother!"

The last translated piece in the envelope is a simple poem. There is no way of knowing if my mother composed this herself or if it was just her sentiments, but I choose to believe from knowing my mother's state of mind during her life time that this poem, whether written by her or not, expressed her true feelings:

Mother, home of my soul,
My heart longs for you.
I wandered near and far,
But never found the peace of home.
Oh, no one of all the strange people
Gave me the peace of home.
Everyone only wants to know his own children,
But does not want to know others.
I have not found anyone
Who understands me as you do;
Who loves me with all the faults
He finds in me.
When I erred and made mistakes
I was heartlessly ignored.
And I felt that only a mother
Can be understanding.
Often, during dark nights
I cried, not understanding.
I did not want to continue this life.
I longed for my mother, my mother always
And felt that my mother
Was the home of my soul.

My grandmother lived to ninety-five; but in her last years she was failing. She had moments of dementia and her physical health was poor. I would imagine that losing my grandmother was truly the saddest day in my mother's life. My mother was never the same after my grandmother passed away. We all loved Omi. My mother lost her best friend and confidante.

CHAPTER 16

My Second Visit with Eva

I called my grandmother Omi because it is German for grandma. We all loved Omi. She was my mother's best friend and closest adviser. It is clear to me now why my mother always listened to Omi without question. My grandmother had saved them both from certain death, and in their struggle my grandmother had become larger than life. I resented the fact that they had such a close relationship with each other that I did not have with my mother. Now I understand why. I was the outsider. But I was loved so deeply. I was everything to my mother. She just was unable to truly trust in our relationship as she did in the love she had with her mother, and I imagine I gave her little reason to trust it. I always rebelled against them. I suppose I was running away from what I could not understand at the time.

I still have so many questions yet to be answered about those days before and after my mother arrived in the United States. How slow the time must have gone while my grandmother anxiously awaited my mother's arrival. Where did they live? How did they pass the time? What was the day like when my mother arrived? I can't even imagine the emotional reunion of these two women so bound together by their love for each other. Why had they missed the opportunity to share these memories with me? Had it all just been too painful to revisit? Eva might have these answers.

These letters are a glimpse into the past, but there are so many gaps. I imagine that a lot of things will never be explained. The woman in the painting still remains a mystery, and what about the family that vouched for my grandmother and my mother? Are there descendants who have more information? If there are, do they even know what their grandfather or great-grandfather did for my family? I have family pictures that show people I don't know and other documents I can't translate. Eva Neisser holds the key to unlock the many doors I still need to walk through. I need another meeting with her. But summer and my fiftieth birthday are approaching. My mother said in her last note to me, "Be good to yourself, Evie." It's my big birthday and she didn't stick around to celebrate with me. So I need to celebrate without her. I need more answers, but I can't focus on this anymore. It is ripping me apart. It will have to wait till fall. Meanwhile, the rest of the papers will just stay in the box.

It is August 4th and I am on a cruise ship on the Baltic Sea. My husband has surprised me with a fourteen-day cruise with my children to Russia and the Netherlands. It is a trip of a lifetime. I am so happy to be with my family, but there is a cloud hanging over me. As much as I appreciate this wonderful trip, my journey to understand my mother has just begun. It is unsettling that I am spending my fiftieth birthday without my mother.

"Mom, why didn't you want to be here to celebrate with me?" I ask. "How could you have left me when you knew I was turning fifty this year? There is such an empty feeling in my heart. Will this pain go on forever?"

I am distracted from my thoughts by David and my children who are telling me to hurry up. We are getting off the ship and having lunch at a fancy hotel in Copenhagen. "David, I see no need to spend extra money on a fancy lunch when we get all these wonderful meals on the ship," I say.

"Come on, don't argue—just enjoy the day," he answers.

But I am shaking inside. I hurt so badly. All the way to the hotel I complain about spending the money for this lunch David has planned. We are outside the restaurant in the lobby of the hotel, but the restaurant appears to be closed.

David says, "Just wait here for a moment with the kids. I'm going to the desk. I will be right back."

I am still complaining to my children when I turn around to see my best friend and her family approaching. I am not sure I believe my eyes. What are they doing here? Have they come to Copenhagen just to celebrate my birthday? That can't be possible. I burst into tears. How had David arranged all of this? So the lunch was just a ruse to get me to the hotel?

"Suzy, I can't believe this!" I scream. "What are you doing here?"

"We are on a cruise that we realized stopped on the same day in Copenhagen. So David and I arranged to meet you for your birthday. Isn't this great?" Suzy answers.

The day is filled with hugs and laughter, and for a short time I forget my sadness. I am with family and friends and it feels wonderful.

Back at home, it is mid-September and the Jewish holidays are upon us. I repeatedly think back to how hard this year has been. The ghosts of my parents and grandparents surround me, and my thoughts return to the box of my mother's papers.

So much time has passed. I have not talked to Eva in months. But the questions are still there. My need to know is still very much alive inside of me. I pick up the phone.

"Eva, it's Evelyn Rauch. I want to thank you again for translating my mother's letters. I am forever grateful. I hope that we can get together again soon. I have many more questions that I hope you can answer. I would love to come visit you again before winter sets in."

"Evelyn, it is lovely to hear from you. How have you been? A happy and healthy new year to you and your dear husband." Eva replies.

"It would be lovely to see you again. Please come for lunch and we can talk."

"How would the end of October be for you? That way the holidays will be over and the weather will still be nice. But I would really like to take you out for lunch," I answer.

"Nonsense, I will make lunch for us. I look forward to your visit. We will talk the week before and confirm."

"Eva, please let me take you out. It would be my pleasure and the least I can do. We can visit for a while at your apartment and then go out for lunch to any place of your choosing," I plead.

"Okay, then I will have dessert at my house ready for after lunch. We will have a lovely visit. See you soon." Eva replies and hangs up.

I open the box containing my mother's papers and various documents and pictures. What should I bring to Eva? I wonder. I can't read the German and I have such a vague idea of the people who are in these pictures. How do I sort through all this and bring what is important? I might leave a precious piece of the puzzle behind and yet I can't overwhelm this eighty-two-year-old woman who is taking up her precious time to help me. I guess I will just take what looks important to me with my little knowledge of German text. I will just have to hope I've picked wisely.

It is a rainy day once again as I travel the monotonous two-hour route to south Jersey and Eva Neisser's home town of Vineland. The sky is darkening with storm clouds as if to say, you are on your way to uncharted territory and opening Pandora's Box once again. I am alone. No David to buffer my anxiety this time. I am filled with uneasy anticipation. Finding out bits and pieces of my mother's and grandmother's past has been a comfort. Knowing that at one time there had been a vibrant, strong, beautiful, and optimistic Steffi makes me proud. It buffers the shame I have felt at times when my mother faltered in public. As I continue this journey, I am convinced I will find more reasons to admire my parents and grandparents.

Eva greets me at her door. "Evelyn, how lovely to see you again. Please let me take your coat. Was the trip from home very long in this nasty weather?"

It gave me time to think of all the things I would still like to ask her. But I don't want her to think that the only reason I come to see her is to drill her for information, so my answer is just a short, "No, the trip was fine."

"So come in, come in. What have you brought for me to look at today? I see you have a folder with you."

"I do have several things that you might be able to help me understand. I am eternally grateful for all your help. It means so much to me to find out my family history. So many of the photographs and papers are a mystery to me. They were obviously very important to my mother for her to have kept them all these years, and now they are even more important to me," I tell her.

"I will do my best, but you know I was also quite young at the time and my memory is not so good anymore. Once your mother came to the United States we only spent several months together. Then your mother and grandmother moved out and went on with their lives."

"But what was my mother like when she was young. Was she pretty" I ask?

"Your mother was very pretty, but there was a sadness in her appearance; a distance, and a nervousness about her. Even in her happiest moments she still seemed anxious. Your grandmother was the eternal optimist, and she tried so hard to make Steffi happy," Eva says regretfully.

At that moment I recall seeing the picture of my mother when she was young that I found among her papers: a sad but beautiful young woman. That sadness never left her.

"What did she do for fun?" I ask hoping to lighten the conversation.

"You can imagine that we had no money in those days. Your grandmother came with ten dollars in her pocket. So we listened to

103

classical music on the radio and took long walks in the park. We were happy to be alive. But a certain element of fear never left any of us. Yet, we all shared a common determination that, because we survived, we would make the most of our lives. Your mother did the best she could to be happy and share good times. In some ways we were all damaged.

"As I told you, once the United States entered the war, my father gave up the business and we moved shortly after that to Vineland. We saw each other very infrequently after that. So I don't know if there is much more information I can provide. I do know that when your mother and grandmother left us they moved to Washington Heights in Upper Manhattan, New York City. Your grandmother continued to work for Liberty Import, the specialty foods company my father started, even though my father no longer worked there. Your mother went to night school to become a baby nurse. Cousin Abe provided the funds for that. She worked in a dress shop during the day in the neighborhood she lived in. Your grandmother also took in sewing to make ends meet. They were very busy piecing their lives back together. They had nothing left, but they were happy to be alive and in this country."

I remember that my grandmother would always do the darning and repairing of socks and clothing in my home as I was growing up. I never understood why because she was so undomesticated in every other way. She really couldn't boil water. Now it makes sense. She had done sewing so long ago for the family and to make extra money.

My mother must have been devastated when my mother-in-law, Grace, became my son's baby nurse. At the time, my mother was recovering from her first damaging brain surgery. Here she had been a baby nurse for so many other strangers and could not help her own daughter. How ironic. My mother's illness had such a devastating effect on our family, but I am beginning to understand that it went deeper than I realized.

"Eva, there are some pictures of people and a painting of someone. I hope you can shed light on their identities."

"Let me see if I know who they are. No, I really have no idea who these people are. Only your great-grandmothers and your grandfather are familiar to me. These other young women I don't know. As I said, I was so young at the time, and in Germany your mother and I were not really friends."

I am getting the distinct feeling the admiration Eva felt for my grandmother was not extended to my mother. I suppose this stemmed back to the family get-togethers in Germany during their childhood, and the fact that my mother was always compared to "those well behaved Berwin girls." I am sure my mother felt completely deflated by these criticisms of her behavior, and so it is conceivable that Eva and my mother had a rather strained relationship. Also, I can imagine that after my mother arrived in the United States my grandmother was probably totally focused on my mother. I am disappointed that Eva isn't able to identify these young women; especially the painting of a young girl dressed in period clothing. It seems very old. It must have had a special meaning since I found it in my room, safely put away in my closet.

"Eva," I begin, "did you ever meet Cousin Abe or any of his family? I wish there was a way I could find out what happened to them. If they still live in Arkansas. I wonder if they know that Abe Goldschmidt saved my mother and grandmother from the hands of the Nazis. I wonder if they were kept in the dark about this story as I was."

"I think it would be lovely if you could find them and let them know that you are the granddaughter of Kathe Lippmann and that Abe saved your mother and grandmother. The Internet might help you with this. It is worth a try," Eva answers. "I myself only had contact with him through the letters I wrote for your grandmother. I became the correspondent and translator for the family when we first arrived here because I could read and write English fluently. But I never met Cousin Abe. I am sure his family would be grateful to find out this story if they don't already know it." Eva looks down at her watch. "Now, I think we should go to lunch. It is noon. I don't drive much anymore, so if you don't mind, I will let you drive and I will direct you."

The streets of Vineland are filled with vacant store fronts. Eva tells me that at one time the town of Vineland was quite beautiful. The main street had been lined with beautiful old trees. For some reason the mayor at the time decided to have all the trees cut down. What was probably a lovely treelined shopping plaza now looked like a vacant ghost town.

"Things change," Eva says sadly. "In the old days we used to love to walk down the avenue, but now it isn't safe."

We place our order at the counter of the luncheonette that Eva has picked out. It is a modest but newly renovated establishment serving deli sandwiches and salads. We sit down at a table and I ask Eva again if there is anything else she can remember about the weeks she spent with my mother and grandmother before they moved away, but she has nothing to add.

So this is it. I have gotten all the information that Eva can provide. I feel empty. I thought this visit would be more productive—that she would remember so many more pearls that I could string together. How I wish that my mother and grandmother had shared their stories with me. Instead I have to piece together what fragments of their life they left to me. I can see that this usually animated lady feels let down as well. There had been so much excitement when she talked to me on my first visit. Then she had a lot to tell me. There is an awkward silence now.

CHAPTER 17

The Missing Chapter: "The Search for Answers Goes On"

The missing pieces to my grandmother's and mother's story are still haunting me. I lie awake at night imagining who the people in the photos are, and how the Goldschmidt's came to Kathe and Steffi's rescue. I have made numerous attempts to locate the descendants of Abraham Goldschmidt. I realize that it would be almost impossible for Abe to still be alive. He would be well into his hundreds. Maybe they could shed light on who Abraham Goldschmidt was. Maybe the story of how he came to save my grandmother and mother from the hands of the Nazis was handed down to them and, if not, might they enjoy and be proud to know that this relative had helped my family escape almost certain death?

The memory of Gerry Goldsmith keeps entering my thoughts. That young dashing man who took me to lunch every so often in the executive dining room of the Pan Am building when I was just in my teens and came to my wedding as one of the only guests. Maybe he is connected in some way to Abraham Goldschmidt. It could be that the reason he had taken such an interest in me while I was growing up was because his family had saved mine. That is why my mother had been so insistent that he be present at my wedding. It all makes sense now.

But how do I find these people? Had Gerry changed his name? Is that why I have not been able to find him in all this time? I have written to various people with the same last name. I have tried to search the Internet for Abe. I've gone through the white pages and the yellow pages looking for anyone with the name Goldschmidt or Goldsmith in the area surrounding Helena, Arkansas. I have written a rabbi and a businessman in Little Rock, all to no avail. I have called the town hall in Helena, Arkansas, but that turned out to be another dead end.

It is Monday morning and I am getting ready to visit my dear friend Gail. I don't know if it is because she too is a second-generation Holocaust survivor that I am reminded of the mystery of Abe Goldschmidt that still plagues me or just that I still need the missing pieces to the puzzle of my family heritage. Whatever the reason, I pick up the phone to call the Helena Town Hall one more time in an attempt at finding someone who knew Abe Goldschmidt. A woman's voice answers, "City Hall Court House."

"This is Evelyn Rauch. I am trying to find out information about a man named Abraham Goldschmidt. He lived in Helena, Arkansas, during the late 1930s and 1940s. Can you help me," I ask?

"I am sorry, but we don't keep those records. That was over sixty years ago," she answers.

"I know it was a long time ago, but it is extremely important that I find out more about this person," I answer.

"Well, you might try calling the Philips County Library—they might be able to help you. They have someone over there who is interested in genealogy," she suggests in a deep southern drawl.

I hang up and dial again.

"Philips County Library can I help you?"

"My name is Evelyn Rauch. I was told that there is someone who might help me with some information about a man who lived in your town in the late 1930s and 1940s."

"The person you want to talk to is Alice Gatewood. Hold on a minute and I'll transfer you to her."

"Hello, Philips County Library," a cheery southern voice answers.

"May I speak to Alice Gatewood, please?" I answer.

"This is she. Can I help you?"

Again I introduce myself. "I am trying to find information about Abraham Goldschmidt who lived in Helena during the 1930s and 1940s. He helped my mother and grandmother escape Nazi Germany. I have been trying for some time to find out more about him and his family as I am doing research into my family history. I hope you can help me."

"I would love to help you," Alice answers. "There are people in this town who don't believe the Holocaust ever happened, and it gets me so angry. It is wonderful that you are looking into this history. There is a woman who is eighty-eight-years old and has lived in Helena her whole life. She knows everyone. This is a small town and people are close. She might have some information on Abraham Goldschmidt. She isn't here today, but she will be in the library tomorrow. I will talk to her and get back to you."

"Thank you so for your help," I reply.

I put the receiver down. I can't believe that I have finally connected with someone who might be able to help me. I can't wait to tell Gail about this. She is the one person who can understand how important every shred of new information about my family is to me.

Gail and I are sitting at the kitchen table. I am telling her all about my conversation with Alice Gatewood. My cell phone rings. I am reluctant to pick it up and interrupt my storytelling, but I am curious so I pick it up and see that it is an area code I am not familiar with.

"Is this Evelyn Rauch?" a male voice on the other end asks.

"Yes," I answer.

Before I can ask who this stranger is, he tells me he is David Solomon, a relative of Abraham Goldschmidt. He quickly rattles off names, dates, and family members and their connections to Cousin Abe. He tells me that Abraham Goldschmidt had no children and that Gerry was Abraham's nephew.

My head is spinning and my jaw drops open. I can't believe that I have finally found someone who is connected with this part of my family history. He is talking so fast and I am still numb from the shock of receiving this call while sitting in Gail's kitchen.

"David," I begin, "do you think you could write this all down for me? I am so excited to hear from you that I can hardly follow what you are telling me."

The reserved, articulate voice on the other end of the receiver says, "I would be happy to draft a letter to you. Please give me your address." We exchange addresses and phone numbers.

I ask the question I have been trying to get an answer to for so long. "Is Gerry Goldsmith still alive? I have been trying to find him."

"Yes, he is very much alive. He lives in Florida and the reason you have not been able to find him is because his first name isn't Gerry—it is Charles. Only his family and close friends call him by his middle name, Gerry. He is listed as Charles G. Goldsmith."

David Solomon recommends that I get in touch with Gerry Goldsmith because he knows much more about the relationship between my grandmother and Cousin Abe. He agrees to send me Gerry's phone number and address.

"This is a small town," he says, "and in those days of the late 1930s and 1940s the Goldschmidt's and the Solomon's worked together to help several families get out of Nazi Germany. We all belonged to the same temple. We were very close, and Gerry and I were in business together. I have a vague recollection that our families helped someone named Kathe Lippmann living in New York."

"That was my grandmother," I answer with tears in my eyes.

"Well, I will get a rambling letter out to you soon."

"David, how can I ever thank you enough for calling? I appreciate your help so much."

I hang up the phone and stare at my friend Gail in disbelief. She has tears in her eyes as well. Her family suffered greatly under the Nazis. We finish lunch and talk about our parents once again and how their lives have impacted ours.

I am home now and I want to call Alice Gatewood and thank her. How had she found David Solomon? I call the Philips County Library once again and Alice answers. "Alice, I just want to thank you from the bottom of my heart for all your help. How did you find David Solomon and how did you know he would know who Abraham Goldschmidt was?"

"Remember I told you there was an old lady who has lived here all her life? She remembered the connection and told me to call David Solomon. I was so excited I called him right away and he called you. You know he is in his late 90s and as sharp as a tack. He still works at his law practice almost every day."

"Alice, I am forever indebted to you. Thank you again so much."

"You are very welcome. When you write a book about all this, send me a copy. I would like it for the library."

How the telephone has played such an important role in my journey. From the day the stranger on the other end of the line said, "You better come to your mother's apartment quickly," to now, so many revelations have come in the form of a phone call. I call 1-800-flowers and send a bouquet to Alice. It's the least I can do for this complete stranger who decided to go out of her way to help me. That is southern hospitality for you!

I can't wait to go to the mailbox and reach in to find David Solomon's letter. It is Monday at 4:30 p.m. and the mail lady is walking up my driveway with the day's mail. It seems there is too much mail to fit in the box. I fumble through the stack of mail and find a letter from David Solomon P.A., Attorney at Law, Helena, Arkansas. I am so excited as I rip open the envelop and find a letter that reads:

Dear Evelyn,
This follows up our conversation of today about the Goldsmith family.
My uncle, Lafe Solomon, was married to Retta Goldsmith Solomon. Retta had three brothers: Abe Goldsmith, Milton Washington Goldsmith, and George Seeman Goldsmith. The latter two were twins. Seeman, as he was known, was the one who had children and they were George Seeman Goldsmith, Jr. and Charles Gerald Goldsmith, who you know as Gerry. Seeman died at an early age and both of his children were quite young. His widow, Sadie, moved to Memphis, Tennessee, and both George and Gerry, the children, spent a great deal of time with Retta and Lafe here in Helena. Ultimately, George and I were responsible for the family operations, but George died at an early age. His widow lives in Amherst, Massachusetts and his three children—two in California and one in Colorado. His widow is Bette Goldsmith.
Gerry is primarily in Palm Beach, Florida. I am in frequent contact with Gerry and we do stay in touch. Gerry has two sons and a daughter; the latter lives in New York City.
It was good talking to you, and if I can furnish any additional information let me know, but I believe Gerry knows more about your family.
My best to you.
Sincerely,
David Solomon

So the next order of business is to get in touch with Gerry. I wonder whether he will remember me. I pick up the receiver and dial. I get an answering machine. I leave a short message explaining who I am and that I hope he remembers my family and me and returns my call. Several days go by. There is no return phone call. So I pick up the receiver once again and call Gerry. This time a familiar voice answers. Even though it has been forty years, this voice I still recognize.

"Hello, is this Gerry Goldsmith?" I ask. "David Solomon gave me your phone number. I am Evelyn Rauch, my maiden name is Mannheimer and my grandmother was Kathe Lippmann. I hope you remember me. I have been trying to find you for a long time. Did you get my message?"

The voice on the other end confirms that indeed he is Gerry Goldsmith and he does remember, vaguely, my grandmother. "Yes, sorry I haven't gotten back to you. I'm running for Mayor of Palm Beach. It has been a very busy time and I just got back from a trip." He continues, "Oh that nice old lady, Katie. I remember her. It has been a long time. May I ask why you are calling me now?"

I get the sinking feeling that Gerry is not as excited to hear from me as I am to contact him. I had built up in my mind that he would be thrilled to hear from me and would want to see me as soon as possible. There is caution in his voice; he is friendly but reserved. My grandmother, Kathe is a vague memory to him. Someone he forgot a long time ago.

"Gerry," I begin, "did you know that Abe Goldschmidt was responsible for saving my family from the Nazis? That he signed the affidavit to bring my grandmother and mother to this country?"

"I knew that our families in Arkansas brought over several families. I was very young at the time," Gerry answers.

"I think somehow Abe was related to my grandmother since her maiden name was Goldschmidt and Goldschmidt is a German Jewish name," I say.

"No, that is not possible. We have been a prominent family in the United States since the Civil War. So you are mistaken about that."

I can tell that the idea that we might be related is agitating him. Does he think I want something from him? "Gerry," I say, "I am just trying to piece together my family history; maybe I will write about it."

"Well, if you do please send me a copy. I would be happy to read it. Nice hearing from you. My daughter is an editor in New York. If you do write something, look her up. Well, I've got to run. Keep in touch."

CHAPTER 18

Going Home to Breslau

The plane is about to touch down in Munich Germany, the first leg of my trip to Breslau—now Wroclaw—Poland. I am returning to my mother and grandmother's hometown. It has been seventy years since Kathe and Steffi fled the Nazis and left Breslau forever. How strange it feels to be in a German plane touching down on German soil as an American second-generation survivor of the Holocaust. I am filled with mixed emotions about coming here. Had I made the right decision to return to this place that my mother and Eva had tried so hard to forget? Eva opened the door to my family history, but I had only a glimpse. As the plane taxis to the gate, I turn to David and say, "Are we crazy to do this?" What if there is truly nothing left of the old Breslau my mother and grandmother knew? After all, it is a Polish town now. I read that most of the city was destroyed during the war.

I want to go home, I think. I feel cold. The icy feeling I had many years ago when I stood at my mother's bedside in the dead of winter of 1999 has returned. I haven't left the plane yet and I already feel threatened. As if something bad is going to happen to us here. I hesitate for just a moment as we leave the plane for the next leg of our journey into the past. Be brave, I say to myself. Your parents had to be brave, so much braver than you are or could ever be. So do this for them and honor their memory by returning to their birthplace and bring closure to their story. Return to say, Hitler may have killed millions of Jews, but he didn't kill us all. And we are brave and will survive and live!

The Munich airport is very white, like the hospital my mother died in; cold and impersonal. We walk what seems like several miles to get to our connecting flight to Wroclaw, Poland. As we travel briskly by the many gates leading to other flights, I am getting the sinking feeling that our flight is not a modern jetliner like the plane we just arrived on from New Jersey to Munich. We have passed all the gates with jets waiting to take off, and now we are descending an escalator to a waiting area that looks out at propeller planes that must be left over from World War II.

"Is that what we are going to fly in to get to Wroclaw?" I shriek. "I didn't come all this way to die in some old bucket and never get to see what I came here for. My parents didn't survive the Nazis for me to come back to Germany and end up dead here. That would be the ultimate irony wouldn't it?"

I must really want to do this pilgrimage because I continue to walk toward the gate knowing that one of the planes out there is destined for Wroclaw, Poland and in a few moments I will be on it.

Once on board it is obvious that we are the only Americans, and most certainly the only Jews. Rugged looking people are sitting all around us. You know the type: stocky, ruddy skin, dirt under the fingernails; the working class of Poland. No one is speaking English. No Americans in their right minds would have gotten on this plane.

As the plane takes off, the sound is deafening. It is so loud that I can't think how scared I am. But I am full of excitement too, and anticipation of what I might discover in Wroclaw, Poland. This is an adventure and I want to be brave.

The plane ride is uneventful, and actually quite pleasant. There are broken clouds and I can see lush farmland beneath us. Instead of the usual pretzel snack you get on a domestic flight in the United States, sandwiches and local beer are being served.

It is only a forty-five-minute flight as it turns out. We touch down on the runway, and I look out into the past. The airport has one runway with an old dilapidated building ahead that must be the terminal since there is no other building in the area. It looks like it is at least seventy-five-years-old.

"I guess there aren't many tourists coming to Wroclaw," I tell my husband.

"Not from the looks of this airport," he answers.

As we exit the plane, there is a cool breeze, a slight chill in the air; I feel shaky and frightened. But I keep it to myself. We enter the terminal and I look around at the faces for someone who could be our guide; that person holding up a sign with our name on it. Something familiar. Something comforting. But there is no one.

So what do we do now? Where do we go from here? We are standing in the terminal with our bags, just standing in the middle of nowhere as people are scurrying around us, finding their way to either private cars or buses with Polish signs. I feel totally lost in another world, almost as if I have left this planet for outer space. Just as I am about to cry, a man with a handwritten sign comes into the terminal with our name on it. We are saved!

"My name is Marcin," he says. Marcin points to the sign, "Rauch."

"Do you speak English?" I ask.

He shakes his head then makes a sign with his fingers to say a little. So now what, I think to myself. We are here for two and a half days, and I specifically made arrangements for an English-speaking guide. What is the use of this person? I guess I will have to address this problem later. First things first: Does he know where our hotel is?

"Art Hotel?" I ask, pointing to my voucher.

He nods. We are on our way! We travel through an area that has seen better days. There are gray cement structures everywhere, much like the buildings we saw on our trip to Russia ten years ago. The cement seems to be disintegrating, and these ugly buildings look as if they are decaying. Not the lovely countryside pictures I saw in Eva's house. This is a totally different landscape. Again I wonder will there be anything left of the town my grandmother and mother knew?

After about a half hour of driving through winding, poorly paved roads we arrive in the town of Wroclaw. Several turns and we are in front of the Art Hotel. I motion to Marcin to come inside. I will ask at the desk if someone speaks English, and then I will ask them to speak to Marcin and find out if he is our guide or if someone else is coming.

The desk receptionist that greets us does not seem very friendly, but she speaks English and agrees to talk to Marcin in Polish and ask him my question. He answers with a smile and nods in my direction.

"Your guide is Tomasz, Marcin is your driver. They will both be here at the hotel tomorrow morning at 8:30 a.m. Is that all you want me to ask?" she says.

"Yes, thank you so much!" I reply with a bit too much exuberance. Marcin smiles.

"See you tomorrow," I say with relief.

The hotel is modest. It looks like it was renovated relatively recently and it seems clean. This is the best hotel in Wroclaw. I imagine they get few American visitors. I am sure no tourists.

We make our way to our room. The room, like the hotel lobby, has been recently renovated. It is quite comfortable. The only thing that seems out of place is a painting on the wall of what looks like Russian soldiers pointing guns with train cars in the background. Not the usual subject matter for a hotel room art piece, but a true reminder of where we are.

We settle in, unpack, and then stroll down to the main square. The weather is cold and raw. The sky has broken clouds and the square is like a movie set. All the buildings are in twelfth and thirteenth century styles, but most of them have been recreated to look like old buildings. They are painted in bright pastel colors and look just like Eva said they would look when she complained about how the Poles had renovated a dignified gray German city and turned it into a circus.

But to me it was quite charming. The square reminded me of the architecture we saw ten years ago in Gda8sk; colorful and sunny; a sharp contrast to the cold, icy winters that plague this part of the world.

There are few retail stores by American standards in the square, but we walk past an old bookstore that looks like it may have been here before the war. So we decide to go in. The store is small, filled with dark wooden shelves with many books in Polish but there are also maps and photo books in German. Behind the counter sits a man who looks like he might be in his eighties. I wonder could he have lived here when this was a German town.

Gutten tag, sprechen sie Englisch? I ask.

"Yes, I speak a little English," he answers. "How can I help you?"

"I am looking to locate several places that existed before the war when this was Breslau. Do you have any maps that might help and could you show us some of the locations I have in this letter?"

"I will try but much of the city has been destroyed and rebuilt. I am not sure what is still standing that you wish to see. But I am still here and so is the store. Tell me the streets and I will get a new map and an old one and we will compare them."

He tells us that he has lived here all his life and that the years during the war were awful. I wonder if he served in Hitler's army or if he was part of the resistance. I will never know. I wouldn't ask. He probably was just a child.

The maps show that a lot of the places I want to see are still in existence. He circles them on the map for me. Also there is a book on Breslau and a photography book of photographs taken of the city from the air before and after World War II. I thank the old gentleman for his help and pay for the map and the two books. These maps will be very helpful in finding the old German streets, which are now renamed in Polish. I will keep these books as a reminder of my mother's and grandmother's home town and all that was lost and destroyed.

We are back in the square again. It is enormous and filled with young people; no one is over thirty. There are outdoor cafes lining the square. We sit down, sample the local beer, and order some unknown food item. We are in my mom's hometown. But how different it must be now from when she lived here. I wish she were here to tell me. I can only guess.

As I am looking at all the young people passing by, it dawns on me that the reason everyone is so young is because those who would be the elders now were massacred. There are very few people left who witnessed what went on here between 1940 and 1945. They either perished from the constant bombing, or were sent to concentration camps where they were murdered or fled to distant lands. Those few who were left must have suffered terribly under Communism, and many could have died from disease and malnutrition.

There is a huge banner that hangs in the square draped over one side of a tall building. It is the map of Poland. On the left side it says Germany and on the right side Russia. I wonder what its significance is.

There is a chill in the air. I am thinking back on how my mother hated the cold. I wonder how she must have felt in the frigid months before she left for England. I imagine that those memories must have laid an icy hand on her heart. Each step into my mother's past brings more clarity to me. I am finally beginning to understand how much she suffered in her lifetime.

My thoughts are interrupted by the waitress who hands us our check and asks if we wish anything else.

The sky is darkening. I check my watch. It is 4:00 p.m. I tell David we better head back to the hotel before it gets any later and we can't find our way back.

It is surreal being here. How far we are away from home and how foreign this place feels. This city has a raw, cold toughness about it, an edgy feel. My mother had that edginess. It was very hard to see behind her tough, critical exterior, but there was such vulnerability underneath; such sadness and pain. This city has that same underlying feel. Something horrific happened here, and the new buildings made to look old can't cover up this killing field.

CHAPTER 19

Tomasz

The phone rings and I slowly open my eyes to focus on the room and where the ringing sound is coming from. Wake up call the electronic machine says as I grab the phone receiver. It's 7:00 a.m. The excitement is already building inside me.

"Get up, David," I bark, "we can't be late today. This is it. This is what I came here for. I want to be on time."

Poor David, he has put up with all my mood changes over these past ten years. He has been patient and kind. But no one can really know how much this trip means to me; how important this single day really is.

We quickly shower and get dressed. Then we head for the hotel dining room where we had dinner the night before. I check my watch: 8:00 a.m. I tell David we only have a half hour for breakfast.

We quickly make our selections from the buffet table and order some coffee. All the time we are eating our breakfast, I am checking my watch. I can't be late. I don't want to miss one minute of this day.

"Okay, David," I say, "that is enough. Time to head to the lobby."

David is still enjoying his breakfast and my watch only says 8:20 a.m.

"Please, Evelyn, calm down. We are only steps away from where we are going to meet Marcin and the guide. Let me at least finish my breakfast," David pleads. I sit glaring at him. Finally he says, "All right already, let's go."

A quick signature on the check and then we are heading for the lobby. As we exit the restaurant, I see Marcin sitting on the couch. He quickly stands up, greets us, and ushers us to the door as another man, slimly built and conservatively dressed, who looks like he is in his early forties, comes through the entrance to the hotel. Marcin motions to him to come over.

As he starts to speak, I can tell he is well educated. He has a soft elegance about him and a gentle, kind manner.

"I am Tomasz your guide for the day," he says. You are Dr. and Mrs. Rauch? I am so happy to meet you. Please follow us so we can start your tour of the city. We have a lot to cover. I have been studying the letter your travel agent sent us that Eva wrote to you. I have tried to map out a detailed itinerary for today so that we can cover all the places you wish to visit. I will try my best to answer all your questions."

"It is wonderful to meet you and thank you so much for preparing for this day," I answer, even though I am mortified that our travel agent forwarded Eva's e-mail rather than just sending a list of what we wanted to see. I had been very clear that Eva's e-mail was private and that I only wanted the agent to use it as a guide to make a list. Eva's e-mail was somewhat critical of how the Poles had restored the city and contained some other derogatory remarks. It reads as follows.

Thanks for your message and good wishes, which I return herein. If you can give me the date of your departure, I will try to send you information on Breslau, Germany, which even today the Poles are not quite sure they will have for the duration. It was German/Bohemian, Prussian from the eleventh century. Your family lived in the southern part, i.e., south of the Ring or Rink now, and since the Russian tanks came in from the south, a great deal was destroyed and replaced by Russian style apartment buildings of the worst possible design, like cell blocks. There is a Jewish synagogue and center that has been rebuilt with the efforts of my generation since 1990, and this should be your first stop. Ask for an English-speaking guide. The elementary school to which I went is still there, at the edge of the South Park, which is also preserved and today, I am told, is a Holiday Inn or Days Inn. You can ask for the former Jewish hospital and the water tower; both are still landmarks. That is another site well known to your family. Your mother went to different schools than I, but I believe she did attend the Jewish eighth grade school next to the destroyed big synagogue called "the Anger" (not angry, but pronounced Ungar, or meadow, lea,), which had those Jewish kids who did not attend the "gymnasium" or accredited pre-university school. I believe your grandparents lived on Viktoria-Strasse, half way between the Rink and the South Park. From there it would not have been far to the cemetery on Lohe Strausse (Lohe is a river into the Oder), which is still preserved because Ferdinand LaSalle, a friend and mentor of Karl Marx, is interred there.. There is this old cemetery, and another one in Kosel, which was where the airport was located way northeast above the Rink. Any guide could point you to these landmarks, which still exist. You would have to look at the Jahrhunderthalle, the largest cupola construction in Europe when built to celebrate the new century in 1900. We used to visit the flower gardens there, but only the very rich people resided there. Do not take a guided tour, they will only show you Bolshevik "panoramas" that the new settlers brought with them in 1949. Hire a taxi and go where you need to go. I don't think anyone can tell you where the IlimingSchule was, that is where your mother went. Your grandmother also often went to a house that still exists next to the Café Fahrig, about four blocks south of the Rink where Dr. Kleemann lived and had his practice. The old café has become something of a landmark. It is opposite the opera house, where your grandmother probably went at least once a month.

You can pull up a map of Wroclaw; there are different squares to paste together. In Polish, Wroclaw is pronounced Rotslaf, which is Wratislavia, or town of Slavic tribes. Breslau is of the same root.

My father's business building still exists and is now next to a hotel, opposite the Elizabeth Church, another place one cannot miss. The yard of the

Elizabeth Church is entered through a twelfth century stone arch called the Kloesseltor, the Dumping Arch, to recall the women who threw hot soup and dumplings on the invading Russians and saved the city from the Eastern Hordes. The part of interest to you is that the right side of the arch has a building attached to it that was the most famous deli in the city, and for a treat your grandmother and mother would have stopped in there for some seeded crescents with Swiss cheese, or lox on rye bread, or creamed herring. It was called the "Kaese-Boehm," Boehm being the name of the owner who specialized in cheeses.

Again, do not take a guided tour, but your own taxi. The Russian Poles have made shambles of a dignified, old, and gray city by painting it light yellow, pink, and purple; an insult to history. If you can find the Jewish Community Center on Google, you might e-mail them and make an appointment to have a guide. Naturally, you will see the mighty river on which we all used to take steamer excursions on Sunday, up to an hour, stopping at some garden restaurant sloping down to the water with music and singing, and then back in the evening.

Take a lot of film along and perhaps some nylons and Columbian coffee for small gifts. Well, that's it. Back to holiday chores. All good wishes to the lucky grandparents!

Eva

"We will start with a quick tour of the streets around your hotel and then from there go to the market square. After that we will drive to the Jewish Center for your 10:30 a.m. appointment. They will show you around and you can ask all the questions you have. We can find out if they have located your grandfather's grave. I hope that they were able to do that. Please call me Tom and ask anything you want to know."

So we start walking down a small ally street, which Tom tells us is where the butcher shops used to be.

"This is the oldest part of the city. The buildings that you see are original and were not bombed. Somehow some of this old city did survive, but nearly seventy percent was destroyed either by the

Germans themselves who destroyed buildings and used the bricks to form barricades to defend the city from the invading Russians, or by the Russians who's unrelenting bombing turned a beautiful city to rubble." Tom tells us remorsefully. "But many of the sites you have asked to see still do exist, remarkably."

Tom continues, "The stalls that once where used to house butcher shops along this narrow street are galleries and souvenir shops now. There is a bronze sculpture at the end of the street of several farm animals that commemorates the former use of these shops."

I am trying to be polite and listen to Tom's detailed explanation, but I am jumping out of my skin wanting to get to the places that my mother and grandmother spent their time in.

We walk by the Saint Elizabeth Church and visit inside to see the renovation that is going on. There are a group of young artisans restoring the frescos; very beautiful and painstakingly detailed work. I begin to wonder if Eva was right in her letter: "Don't take a guided tour, take a cab and go where you want." Are we just wasting precious time?

We reach the market square, which is quite impressive. I had truly been awestruck by it yesterday when we first saw it. But it was not the same as when my mother walked here. It is a Polish city now with brightly colored buildings not the gray, dignified place Eva described. I ask Tom why the buildings are painted in these pastel colors.

"Before the Germans took over Wroclaw and named it Breslau, the houses were painted these colors. The Poles just renovated these buildings and restored them to how they looked originally."

I wonder if Eva knows this fact. And if not, would that have altered her bitterness about the change in color? So much in life is perception. Tom tells us that just one side of the square is original. Everything else has been rebuilt to look original.

"Breslau was the last strong hold of the Third Reich. The city was rendered a ghost town after 1945 and it took years for people to return. Seven hundred seventy thousand people fled, only two hundred thousand remained in the city. Thousands died trying to flee. They were either crushed to death by the panicking crowds or died from exposure and starvation. Those who stayed had a similar fate. The reason there are so few older residents is because the Germans either died or did not return. The people living here now are from the east and are the new settlers of Wroclaw," Tom explains.

I ask, "What is the meaning of the large red banner that covers most of that four-story bank building on the right side of the square? It is so prominent."

"As you can see there is an outline of the city. In the left upper corner it reads Germany and on the upper right side is written Russia. This is to remind the Poles that Germany and Russia both have occupied this city and to always work hard to protect it and defend it from invaders. The Poles are never secure in the belief that this will always remain Polish land. It has changed hands so many times."

So that explains Eva's true dislike for the Polish people. Not only were the Poles terrible to the Jews, they retook the city that she considered German. How can you blame her for her true hatred of the Poles? I understand now how she can never return for a visit to this place. The scars are too raw.

It is hard to imagine how horrific the years from 1938 to 1945 were and even beyond when the city was so devastated. I am glad my mother and grandmother got out of Breslau before the total devastation took place. I imagine that Kristallnacht had to have been frightening enough.

Somehow, even though I have read so much and watched films of World War II, being here helps me to understand the suffering so much better; it brings the enormity of it all home, and yet the streets are wiped clean of the blood that was shed here. There are few traces of the past. People are laughing, shopping, and having coffee in the sidewalk cafes. Only the red banner looms over the square as a constant reminder that something terrible happened here. Never forget.

Tom continues to speak about the buildings, the town hall, and the beer cellars located in the square; but my mind is elsewhere. My inner clock is ticking and I can't control my emotions. I can feel my pulse as tears well up in my eyes. How could I have been so blind to all this? I am beginning to really understand why my parents never spoke about their past. It had been obliterated. Whatever they once knew is no more; gone in a sea of destruction. Of course they wanted to move on. There was no way to go back.

My thoughts are interrupted as Tom asks me if I have any questions. If not, he says we'll return to the car and head to the Jewish Center for our appointment.

Tom tells us that Marcin is waiting for us in front of the hotel and from there it is about a ten minute drive to the Jewish Center. I check my watch to see that it is 10:15 a.m. We are right on schedule. In just a few short minutes I will finally meet Justyna and add a face to the voice that answered the phone when I called to make this appointment at the Jewish Center.

I followed Eva's advice and searched the Internet for a phone number for the Jewish Community Center in Wroclaw. It proved to be a more difficult task than I had imagined. There was no site in English, and I could not decipher the phone number. After several attempts to e-mail the site, I finally got a response and a phone number to call. The woman who answered the phone was Justyna. She was very polite, but somewhat reserved. She must have been quite curious about why I was calling the center. As I have come to realize, few Westerners seem to travel to this part of the world. I told her at the time that I was trying to trace my mother and grandmother's roots. I would like to see the White Stork Synagogue that I had read about and hoped she could arrange for a tour. I think my grandparents may have been members of this synagogue. I also asked if they would be able to research where my grandfather's grave might be.

Once Justyna realized what my motivation for this call was, she softened her tone and was most helpful. "I will start a search for your grandfather's grave," she offered.

She said she would arrange for a tour of the White Stork Synagogue, but that it was under renovation and we could only see the outside. When I asked her about the renovation and what was being done to the synagogue, her voice reached a high pitch and in a burst of exuberance she answered, "Everything!" A series of e-mails ensued after that. We set this date and time for my appointment.

The facade of the Jewish Community Center is unobtrusive. We almost drive past it. Just a few Hebrew words above the doorway tell us that we are in the right place. We are escorted in. The inside of the center is unassuming much like the exterior. There is a small glass counter with some Jewish artifacts and book shelves with a sparse amount of books. Sitting behind the counter is a young, attractive woman who looks like she is in her thirties.

"May I help you?" she asks in Polish."

"I am looking for Justyna Molassy. I am Evelyn Rauch and this is my husband, David. Do you speak English?" I ask.

A broad smile lights up this dark haired, engaging young woman's face.

"I am Justyna Molassy. Welcome to the Jewish Community Center of Wroclaw."

She comes around the counter and gives me a strong handshake. I want to give her a big hug but I am afraid she will misunderstand such a show of emotion.

Justyna continues, "I am so happy to meet you. How was your trip to get here? Did you find the center all right? Can I get you anything to drink?"

"We are fine and so excited to be here and to meet you," I answer.

Justyna tells us that she has arranged for a tour of the community center and the temporary prayer room that they are using while the temple is being rebuilt. Again she expresses her apologies for not being able to let us inside the temple.

I am not sure whether to take this risk of angering her, but I decide that it is important enough; I am not coming back here and I want to see with my own eyes everything I can. So after a long pause I plead, "Is there any way we might be able to take just a peek inside? We won't disturb anything. Please? We have come such a long way."

Justyna turns toward a man who has been sitting very quietly on the far left side of the center. I hardly notice him until Justyna starts to speak to him. She speaks in Polish and he answers her then approaches us. He is a man, I imagine, in his late fifties, short with a scruffy beard, wearing a brimmed cap. He reminds me of many pictures I have seen of Eastern European Jewish refugees. His face is sullen. The many years of hardship scar his face and he walks slowly and deliberately.

"This is your guide, Jerzy Kitchler," explains Justyna. "He is one of our temple members and chairman of the board of the Association of the Jewish Religious Communities. He makes the decisions as to who can enter the temple at this time. I've asked him if he will let you take a quick look inside the synagogue and he has agreed. He speaks a little English, so he will take you now on a tour of the center and the synagogue. When you finish the tour you will come back here and we will try to find your grandfather's grave. So far I have had no luck locating it, but there is a man who will be here shortly who might be able to help us. So go now. I will be waiting for you at the end of the tour."

All this time Tom has been standing with us silently. He seems to be very moved by all of this. He is just a quiet, reserved man trying to understand the importance of this visit. I am hoping he can be a good translator so I can make the most of this moment.

After some more introductions, handshakes all around, and a brief explanation of how Jerzy came to Wroclaw and the White Stork Synagogue by way of the Ukraine in the 1950s, we begin to walk toward an archway leading to a courtyard. The synagogue is beyond the courtyard.

In broken English, Jerzy tells us that during the deportation of the Jews thousands were herded into this courtyard. Many were crushed to death before they even made it to the trains to be sent to the death camps. There was no food or water.

The courtyard is small in size compared to the synagogue that stands beyond it. The four of us standing in this courtyard almost fill it. One can hardly imagine how thousands could have been herded into this space. It must have been horrific, such a terrible human tragedy.

Jerzy Kitchler leads us through the courtyard, past the synagogue, and into a side building. His short, bent silhouette slowly and deliberately ascends a steep stairway. At the top of the steps he turns right and stands in front of two imposing doors. He reaches into his pocket for a large key ring then opens the doors to reveal a modest but beautiful prayer room. It has been here for so many years providing a sanctuary for so many during troubling times in history. It has a true aura of peace and tranquility and I feel my voice shrink to a whisper so as not to break the silence. I walk quietly up to the alter. There are several Torahs in the ark, they must have survived Kristallnacht. I imagine they were hidden underground. The fact that this place of worship still exists in what was once part of Nazi Germany and then the Iron Curtain is a true miracle.

Jerzy tells me that during the years of occupation by the Russians, the Jews, or what remained of them, were driven out. Only after the Russians left did a small number of Jews return.

How brave these people are to stand their ground and fight for the freedom to practice their religion in such a hostile environment, I think. How much I have taken for granted in my own life. But how could I know? Why had no one enlightened me? Or was I just not listening? I don't really know.

Jerzy asks if I am ready to leave, and when I nod yes, he leads us out of the sanctuary and again takes the large key ring from his pocket and locks the door behind us. He is the gatekeeper and I can tell he takes great pride in watching over this holy place.

We descend the long, steep stairs again and now we are back in the courtyard.

Jerzy Kitchler turns to Tom and speaks to him briefly in Polish.

"He will take you inside the White Stork Synagogue," Tom says. "But you have to be very careful. We will stay for only a moment."

Again Mr. Kitchler reaches into his pocket for the large key ring and slowly, with the utmost respect, he opens the door to the synagogue. "Please watch your step," he says as we enter the vestibule.

I feel tears on my cheek. I am witness to a rebirth of a battered but not destroyed ideal. This temple is rising up from the ashes of the Holocaust, and even though there are only four hundred Jews that will worship here, it is a symbol of what is possible.

The sanctuary is so impressive, rising several stories high, with many arches and a gallery upstairs for the Jewish women. It is an orthodox synagogue. Women sit separately from the men. The decorations are painted in the archways where, in former times, they were probably embellished in gold or brass. But the grace and beauty of the sanctuary is not diminished and it takes my breath away. I can hear the Shamah! I can hear my ancestors praying. I have stepped back into my history; my roots and I will never be the same.

Jerzy tells Tom in Polish that it is time to go. He is afraid someone will get hurt. So Tom turns to me and says in such a kind way, "Mrs. Rauch, if you are finished reflecting then we should move on to our next stop as to not miss anything you have come to see."

In these few hours that I have spent with Tom I have realized that what happened here in Eastern Europe affected everyone and continues to effect all generations to come. The Holocaust happened here: terrible suffering, terrible and unthinkable brutality, and yet the human spirit wants to survive, wants to soar, wants to be happy and fulfilled. Some want to say what happened here never happened, some want to sweep it under the rug and move on. But there are others like Tom who are truly moved by what happened here and want to make amends.

We start walking back to the entry door of the temple and I turn to take one last look, one brief moment to make a memory forever.

The door closes and we are in the courtyard again and a cool drizzle is dampening the air. It is October but the winter is whispering that it is approaching. Winters must be brutal here. How it must have felt to be standing in this courtyard in the dead of winter waiting for the transports to take Jews to the death camps.

Justyna is standing in the doorway of the Jewish Center. She approaches and tells us that they have not located the grave in the cemetery near the airport, which is where ninety percent of the Jews of Breslau were buried.

"The Germans kept exceptional records," she says. "If your grandfather was buried there we would have found a record of the grave."

I tell her that it is more likely that Ernst was buried in the old Jewish cemetery inside the city on Slezna Street since it was my understanding that my grandmother would walk to the cemetery every day to sit and reflect.

"Unfortunately, there are no records for this cemetery," Justina tells us regretfully. "But you will go and make a search. I wish you success in finding your grandfather's grave and I am so glad to have met you. I wish you a safe and happy trip. Please keep in touch and let me know how the rest of your trip turns out."

This time Justyna reaches out to give me a warm hug. I have made a friend in Wroclaw, Poland.

Outside the weather is still cold and damp. Marcin is standing by the car ready to open the door for us. Tom leads the way and tells us that the next stop will be the south side of town where my mother lived. He says that is where we will find the cemetery and most of the places I want to visit. The actual building and street is no longer there, but the area called the South Rink is still in existence and the school that my mother attended and the park, South Park where she played and took long walks with my grandmother are still there.

"We'll drive to the old Jewish cemetery first," Tom says.

We drive about ten minutes and stop in a small parking lot.

"This is as far as we can drive. From here we have to go on foot to the entrance to the old Jewish cemetery," Tom explains.

As I start to walk toward the large gate that is several hundred yards ahead of me, I begin to feel a deep sense of loss, an ache that tears at my heart; a sadness that cannot be measured and a true empathy for those who suffered so terribly. I am deliberate in my step. My feet tread ever so lightly on this ground. I feel the earth tremble beneath me and yet everything in reality is still.

We enter the gates and Tom asks the grounds keeper if he has any record of an Ernst Lippmann who died in 1927. He has no record, he tells Tom in Polish. Tom tells us that the man says we are free to walk through the cemetery and try ourselves to find the grave.

I look around at a sight that I am sure to never forget. So hard is this sacred place to describe. There is a heavy mist in the air, a cool, chill, and damp breeze; it whispers of secrets that are too horrible to comprehend. The trees, heavy with wet, deep forest green leaves, look as though they are weeping. The gravestones are bent, tossed, toppled, and violated. Names are defaced, brass and gold ripped from their anchors. The ivy is so thick that it forms a velvet carpet over the gravestones and the floor of the cemetery; a blanket to hide the identity of those who have perished.

I am silent next to David and Tom as I walk ever so slowly past row after row of ivy-covered graves, hundreds of markers with no mark. I turn to Tom and say, "I don't think there is any way I can actually identify my grandfather's grave."

Tom looks at me with such kindness in his face. In his eyes I can see tears held back only by the wells of his lower lids. "I will help you look," he says. "Don't give up yet."

We walk row after row, grave after grave. As we step deeper and deeper into the heart of the cemetery, we are enveloped in a sea of deep green ivy. Everywhere we turn there are hidden, unidentifiable graves. Tom walks briskly ahead of me now, trying at times to push the heavy foliage away from the stones it covers; desperately trying to find that needle in a haystack, that illusive name: Ernst Lippmann.

"Tom," I plead, "it's okay. I don't need to find the actual grave. I can feel my grandfather's presence. I know he is here. I can hear his whisper. His soul is sleeping in this place of decaying beauty."

"But you can't give up. I know we will find it," he begs. But his voice is questioning.

"It's okay, Tom. I am at peace. I know I have found my grandfather. I know he knows I am here. It's okay," I say trying to make him understand. I am okay. I am at peace.

Reluctantly, Tom consents to give up the search. I sense his disappointment is greater than mine.

"We can go now," I say gently.

We walk slowly back toward the gate of the cemetery. I turn to take one last look into a garden of forgotten souls. But I will never forget, not ever.

"Thank you, Tom," I say. "Thank you for your help."

We return to the car in silence. What is there left to say? Once in the car Tom turns to me, again with such compassion he asks, "Are you ready to go on? Do you need more time before we continue?"

"No, I am fine. I want to see everything," I answer.

"Then we will move on to visit the old Jewish hospital buildings, which are still being used, but will soon be closed because a new hospital is being built. This is where your grandfather died according to what I can figure out from your family history," Tom says. "It is close to the street your grandparents lived on. Would you like to get out and walk around?"

David and I get out and walk the rather narrow alleyway between the buildings. We take some pictures and talk about what it must have been like to be a patient in this hospital that seems so archaic. No wonder he died of gangrene after a simple hernia operation.

These buildings also remind me of the antiquated Columbia Presbyterian Hospital where my mother underwent brain surgery. It was a true hellhole. And I still have nightmares over the patients screaming in the paint peeling halls. I remember when my mother could not eat and she was drowning in her own saliva. The doctor kept her on a liquid diet. She developed pneumonia because she had no gag reflex and she kept aspirating the liquids. I begged the nurses to stop feeding her, but they said the doctor ordered liquid meals for her. I made numerous attempts to contact him, but he never returned my calls.

"Where to next?" I ask as we climb back into our car.

"South Park and the school your mom attended. The ride to South Park follows the Oder River."

Eva told me that on Sundays her family and the Lippmann family took boat rides on the river and stopped for lunch on its banks at a riverside café. There is still a faint mist and cool chill in the air. Not a good day for a boat ride. But as we travel along the banks of the Oder River I can visualize how lovely a bright, sunny Sunday afternoon could have been taking a slow sail down the river. How lovely it must have been to stop and have an elegant lunch with a small quartet playing music and possibly singing.

Tom interrupts my daydreams when he tells us to look to our right. "This is the building that was your mother's school. It is now a library, but I am pretty sure this is the building described in Eva's letter."

It almost looks like my elementary school but there is still barbwire around it.

"South Park is just ahead, would you like us to stop and walk around?" Tom asks.

"Yes, please," I answer.

As we walk through the park grounds, Tom tells us that in the summer there are musical events in the park. I can imagine that my mother and grandmother must have spent a great deal of time here. The park is still beautiful with several ornate footbridges crossing over small brooks and a pond with a fountain and rowboats. The paths are treelined and there are many benches along them.

I can visualize my mother and grandmother taking a stroll through the park and stopping to sit on a bench and listen to some music. Music was such an important part of their lives. It was the thread that wove their relationship. The love they shared for music deepened the love they felt for each other. I never understood music the way they did. Only now, as I grow older, have I developed an interest in classical music. In some ways the beautiful sounds of the orchestra have helped to heal the deep wound I feel inside. When I listen I can hear my mother's voice.

Tom looks at his watch. "We probably should continue on so that you can see everything you still wish to see and maybe stop for a late lunch or pastry near the opera house."

I realize that we have been going nonstop and I haven't given a thought to whether Tom might be hungry and in need of a break.

"Tom, lets visit the opera house next if it is not too far away?" I ask.

"Okay, we'll visit the opera house and then have some lunch, or we can just stop for pastries at the café across the street that Eva wrote about in her e-mail," Tom answers with some relief in his voice.

The opera house is beautiful, painted in deep yellow and white with touches of gold in a baroque style. It takes up a full city block. Somehow falling bombs did not destroy this beautiful building. It is hard to imagine how it escaped destruction. It stands alone with very little to protect it. We walk inside, but the main music-hall doors are locked, and so we cannot see inside. The ticket window is open, however, and I wonder if we might be able to get tickets for the opera tonight.

"Tom, would it be all right if I just asked if there might be tickets available for tonight's performance?"

"Go right ahead," Tom says. "I will wait for you outside."

"Pardon, do you speak English?" I ask the woman at the box office.

"Yes. Can I help you?" the woman answers in perfect English.

"Do you have a performance tonight, and if so, what opera will be performed?" I ask. "Are there seats available?"

"There is a performance tonight. It is the opera *Nabucco*, and yes, there are seats available. Would you like to purchase some?" she asks as she hands me a brochure. "*Nabucco* is the story of Nebuchadnezzar and the Jews. If you would like I can print out the libretto in English for you."

I can hardly contain myself. I turn to David to ask, "Please, can we go tonight?"

"Of course, I wouldn't miss it for the world," he says.

"Then two tickets, please. The best you have," I say to the lovely woman behind the counter.

"I only have the last row in the orchestra, but it is in the center section," she says regretfully.

"We'll take them," I answer without hesitation.

Outside Tom has been waiting patiently all this time. "Were you able to get tickets?" he asks.

"Yes," I answer with great joy. "I am so excited!"

"That is wonderful! I know you will enjoy the opera," Tom says. "And now let's go across the street to Café Fahrig, the pastry shop Eva wrote about. It is still there. It has been on this corner for over one hundred years. It used to extend to the end of the street, but after the war the shop was made smaller."

The café is small, just a few tables and chairs to sit and have a cup of coffee. But beyond the tables are two glass cases filled with all kinds of sumptuous pastries. It is hard to make a decision on which one to have, and since this is going to be our lunch I want to make the right choice.

"Go ahead Tom," I say, "order something good for yourself. What would you suggest for me?"

But before he can answer I know already what I am going to have: a cream puff. My grandmother's favorite. That's it. I wait for Tom to place his order and then I ask him to order me one cream puff. I remember how much Omi loved them. She had taken me many times to a similar looking café on Seventy-Second Street on the west side in New York for cream puffs when I was a little girl. She always ordered extra whipped cream. "Bitte mehr schlagsahne," she would say. A cream puff never tasted so good as this one. It is decadent and sweet and filled with all my memories of those Sunday afternoons with Omi rapped up into one big cream puff.

The big glass windows at the front of the shop look out on the opera house across the street and I allow my mind to wander back to the 1920s when my grandmother and grandfather came to listen to music and enjoy a good cup of coffee and some Danish. I can almost hear them talking.

I pick up the libretto and start to read the synopsis of the opera we are going to see. In short it tells the story of the plight of the Jews as they are assaulted, conquered, and subsequently exiled from their homeland by the Babylonian King Nabucco (in English, Nebuchadnezzar). The historical events are used as the background for a romantic and political plot. How ironic and appropriate that this is the opera that is being performed tonight. How the Jewish people have been persecuted over the centuries but nothing, absolutely nothing, could compare to the Holocaust.

I look at my watch and it glares back at me: 3:30 p.m. Only an hour and a half left till we have to say good-bye to Tom.

"If we hurry we can still see the university and the bridge of locks," Tom tells us.

These are more of the sights I imagine Eva told me to avoid. But Tom has been a prince about showing me everything I wanted to see. How could I tell him I did not want to go to these places that he had picked out? After all, he is proud of his hometown, and I need to respect that. So we return to the car. Marcin is waiting and we drive along a wide boulevard. Tom points out the cupola and the botanical gardens that Eva mentioned.

I guess that is it: one day's worth of sightseeing to explain a lifetime of sadness and regret. But this day has answered a lot of questions for me. It has made me understand my mother's deep depression: the loss of her homeland; all that was familiar, all that was comfortable and safe. So much time has passed since my mother and grandmother fled to save their lives. But the remnants of their past is still here. Breslau may have been bombed to smithereens, but some things have survived to whisper, we Jews lived here. No amount of paint and polish can wipe away the sad history that Wroclaw has. I will never forget. I am changed forever!

From Wroclaw we fly back to Munich to meet friends for a week long river cruise down the Danube. Our itinerary takes us through the very heart of what was once Bavaria and the Eastern Bloc. Because we are all interested in the Jewish history of the places we are touring along the river, we have arranged for guides who are well informed in this area. In each city or town as we ask questions about the Holocaust and anti-Semitism, it is becoming apparent to me that anti-Semitism in Eastern Europe is alive and well. Each guide sadly admits that anti-Semitism is on the rise once again. What is it about this part of the world that breeds such hatred? I wonder.

The scenery that unfolds before my eyes is beautiful. But what lies under the carpet of velvety green rolling hills? The wind echoes of dead souls and unspeakable horrors. I feel uneasy.

We reach the town of Melk. I strike up a conversation with a man who tells me he is from the mid west in the United States. He is a tour guide and has arranged a Mozart tour down the Danube River. He has an accent that sounds German or Austrian. This friendly gentleman points to a monastery with a large clock tower that we are going to tour today. "See up there," he says. "From that balcony you can see the concentration camp I was imprisoned in during the war. You can hardly make it out from here, but the remnants of it are still there. I think I will just stay on the boat today."

The next stop is Budapest. Our fifty-year-old guide tells us that, until she was forty, she had no idea she was Jewish. Her father hid this information from her for fear of further persecution by the Russians after the war. He had been imprisoned in a concentration camp and was one of the few Jews liberated in 1945 who stayed in Budapest, Hungary. He told her all of this on his death bed. I can tell that she is still struggling with her identity and is reluctant to talk much about it for fear of retribution. Growing up under Communism must have been very tough.

We visit the beautiful synagogue in the heart of Budapest that has been restored, but it is mostly a museum. Of the half a million Jews who lived in the city before the war, only four hundred are left.

In every town we visit it is the same: the synagogues are restored, but there are no Jews to worship in them. Hitler's plan was to preserve the artifacts of an extinct Jewish race, and as I see it in this part of the world, he succeeded.

CHAPTER 20

Leaving a Legacy

It is 10:30 p.m. and I am sitting beside my sleeping husband. We are on our way home from our trip to Eastern Europe. The plane cabin is dimly lit and most of the passengers are asleep, but not me. I am wide awake with my thoughts and all of the snapshots in my mind of the town my mother grew up in. It is such a long way from where I grew up in New York City with its tall modern buildings, its fast pace and energy. My mother's childhood was so different from mine. Everything about our lives was and is different. The United States—its freedom, its vastness, its cultural diversity, and its climate—is the exact opposite of that which was once Nazi Germany and now Poland. My parents and grandmother knew all this, and yet they never shared that knowledge with me. I suppose it was their way of protecting me. They never wanted me to know the tyranny of a dictatorship that they had experienced. And yet in the end I am their daughter and granddaughter. I had to know. And at the end of my mother's life, she also knew this. She wanted me to understand what happened to her and now I do.

The hours of my journey home are ticking by slowly as I reflect not only on my trip to Poland, but my journey of self-discovery. It has been painful as you know now. But to be enlightened is never a bad thing. It is how we grow and change and get to be better human beings. So this is the legacy my parents and grandparents left to me.

I close my eyes and my mother's voice calls to me. "Write my story, Evie. Write my story."

I am confused and scared. I am not a writer. Why should I write this? Isn't it enough for me to know where my roots are? I get it, Mom. Isn't that enough?

And then in a rush of emotion as the tears come running down my face I realize it is not enough. My children have to know this story. They have to know their roots. This is their heritage not just mine. My father said to me a long time ago when I was a teenager growing up in the safe environment of Riverdale, New York, "When they put you in a line and tell you to go left and the others to go right, you better know who you are and where you came from."

I know who I am now, but do my children have any idea? What will they find in my top draw when I am no longer alive? This story will most certainly be in there. But what about me will I leave to them? My life is wrapped up in my mother's story because without knowing it my life has been so deeply affected by what happened to my family. My children's lives have been and will forever be influenced by my journey through life.

I imagine my paintings will be of interest to them. Many of which are of people and places I have visited and photographed. Some of the paintings are representations of subjects in the photos my son took, the true photographer in the family. So in this way we are connected by the subjects we choose to interpret and immortalize. I imagine that the photos from this trip will also be in that draw; also the albums of photos of my trips when I was young. I love to travel and so did my mom. But this book that I need to write will truly define who I am and what my family faced during our darkest hours. Why is it that tragedy always brings out the spirit in all of us and that until we have suffered great loss the true meaning of life is not evident to us? If we could only have this wisdom without the suffering.

But what else can I leave them to know who their mother is? I don't have heroic stories of my own to tell. Maybe just some letters, just like my mother left me; just some stories about a girl who just wanted to be happy and raise a family. Who would have ever thought that the essence of who I am would have been so tied up in my heritage? But the best way to understand me is to understand Steffi because she had such an impact on who I have become. The gift she gave me I can only pass on.

I close my eyes now. When I open them again we are back in the States. It seems surreal; as if we never left. I need to write all this down before I forget!

EPILOGUE

Writing Nonfiction: No Experience Necessary

The clock is ticking on. Several years have gone by since I received Eva's note and I began my journey of discovery into my mother's and grandmother's past. I have made several attempts to begin writing their story. It has not gone well. Each piece seems a feeble attempt at recreating a timeline rather than bold and powerful storytelling.

How do I begin? I am overwhelmed by this task and each time I sit down to write, my emotions get the better of me and I crumble. I am stuck and the frustration of my ineptness to tell this story is maddening. Each time I begin, sheer terror wells up inside me. I relive those horrible days in January of 1999 and I can't continue.

What to do? Most of the time I just give up, return the box of papers and photographs to the closet, take a deep breath, stand up from the computer, and walk away. But I have to do something with this story. It was left to me to tell. It is my responsibility to my family. How ironic that in life my mother never trusted me to do the right thing, and now that she is dead, I can't seem to bring myself to do this. Maybe she was right all along. Maybe I am incapable of many things. I think I will go mad if I don't find my way through this. But maybe I am really not up to this challenge.

At first it was having the emotional distance of time from my mother's suicide to be able to even look at her papers. Then it was the frustration of not knowing what all these important papers meant.

147

And now it is facing the fact that I am incapable, once again, of pleasing my mother. Once again I am letting her down. I need more tools. But where do I get them is the $64,000 question, as my mother would say.

It is a Monday afternoon, and as I always do like clockwork, I walk to the mailbox to get the day's mail. The usual junk mail and bills await me, but there is also a large white envelop from Cornell University.

I remember my children walking up to this mailbox, each of them in their own time, when they were waiting so hopefully for an acceptance letter from Cornell. I stared at them from the window; neither of them wanted me to accompany them. They each stood at that mailbox for what seemed like forever. And then there was pure joy on their faces as each opened the letter that they had waited for: "We are happy to inform you that you have been accepted for the following semester as a student at Cornell University." I bounded out the door to meet Eden, who is my first born, and the two of us hugged and jumped for joy. Then we realized we were locked out of the house in our bathrobes. With Jeff I checked the door before I ran out, a little less spontaneous, but still heartfelt. Each had gotten their wish and I had accomplished what my mother had always wanted for me, but I had let her down. My kids were going to Cornell University.

Here I am at that same mailbox holding this large white envelope from Cornell University that is addressed to me. Inside is a catalogue for their summer adult education program, CAU. I walk back to the house with no idea whether to just toss this as another piece of junk mail or thumb through it just to see what they offer.

I have taken courses at Cornell once before. One year when my daughter was taking summer classes there, I took courses for two weeks so I could spend some time with her. The first one was a baking class, which David and his sister Linda also took. We spent a lot of time throwing flour at each other, but we had fun. The second week I took a sculpture course that I loved. Eden had very little time for me that summer. She was taking a very intense chemistry class and she spent most of her time in the library and in the chemistry lab, so I had lots of time to roam the campus. It was so beautiful at Cornell, particularly in the summer. All the gorges and the trails surrounding the university were breathtaking. I understood then why my mother had wanted this experience for me. So now at least for a brief moment in time, I too had come to study at Cornell University.

The phone rings. It is David telling me he will be home soon and I can get dinner ready. I toss the mail on the counter. It is time to focus on dinner.

Several days go by. I am standing in the kitchen and the white envelope catches my eye under a pile of more unread mail. I open the envelope and start thumbing through the pages of summer courses offered. One course jumps out of the catalogue: Writing Nonfiction: No Experience Necessary. Maybe this is my chance to find a way to write my family story, I think. I will talk to David, and if the timing works out for this summer, I will take this course.

I call the CAU office. There is limited space in the class so I must act quickly. No time to think much about this. "Okay," I say, "sign me up."

Several weeks later a packet from CAU arrives. I quickly open it to find a congratulatory letter that I am accepted into the summer writing class and a list of instructions.

Well, now I have to take the course. It is hard to sleep. I am scared to make this bold step into this unfamiliar territory. Each day I try to write something relevant and profound about the events that took place in my mother's life, but the words sound empty and dispassionate. I begin again but nothing changes. My confidence is eroding.

It is Saturday morning in early July. The sun is shining. Today is the day I am leaving for Cornell. The ride to Cornell is a familiar one. I have done it so many times during the six years my children went to the university. I remember my ride to see Jeffrey after my mother died and how much seeing him had helped me. Now I am hoping that what I am doing will somehow help him in his life. That knowing his rich heritage will embolden him as well as Eden. I am optimistic that somehow Cornell will enlighten me, too, and I will find my path through this story.

I am about forty-five minutes from Cornell now. As I continue my drive I think back to my first trip up here after my own college days. Eden and I went to Cornell for her first interview. It was a beautiful sunny day, much like today, in October of 1986. We took a tour of the campus. The trees were ablaze with color. Only a few leaves had dropped. Our tour guide was an engineering student. He told us to take a good look around us. How beautiful the campus was in the shining sunlight. How warm the temperature was for mid-October. How all the leaves where colored brightly but none had fallen. Then he said again take a real good look because in the four years you spend here you will never see a day like this again. We all laughed, but truer words were never spoken. The weather at Cornell is always less than perfect. I suppose that the cold and damp winters make for good study habits. The summers at Cornell can be brutal. My kids rarely complained about the weather, but I remember my own college days at nearby Syracuse University and how I traipsed through the snow carrying my heavy black port-folio that was almost larger than me. I had spent several brutally hot summers at Syracuse University trying to complete college in three years. I even remember one summer when it snowed in July. You could never predict what Mother Nature had in store. But the weather made me tougher and more determined to complete my education in three years.

Also, I wanted to finish college quickly so I could come home and marry David. My parents did not approve of this idea and made it very clear that if I wanted to get married that young I better be able to stand on my own two feet because they were not going to support me. I remember working two jobs while taking twenty-five credits in order to save money and graduate early. I designed and decorated the windows of Casual Corner, an upscale ladies clothing store off campus. My boss was a tyrant, but I put up with him because I made $35 a week, which was a very good salary for part-time work in those days. The nights I had free from school work I would baby-sit for a college professor of mine. The standard joke in my college dorm was if you had to stay up late to study you would have company because Evelyn was always up in the lounge doing some project. I rarely slept in my college days. There was also the ever-looming heavy air of illness that surrounded me all my life and was ever-present in my college days. My father was failing. I suppose I always had a sense of urgency to get home as fast as I could. Dad's clock was running out and I knew it.

I arrive at north campus, where students are waiting eagerly to direct us to registration at Court Hall. I can't believe that I am really here. I am scared; so scared I can feel my heart pounding in my chest. I pick up my packet and head for the graduate dorm on north campus, Ecology House, which will be my home for the next week.

How ironic that I am at Cornell taking a writing course. Here, where my children spent their college days; where I faced my son for the first time after his grandmother's death. The school my mother had dreamed I would someday go to. Here is where I have come to learn how to tell her story.

I am sitting in the Hollis E. Cornell Auditorium in Goldwin Smith Hall listening to a welcome speech for all CAU participants. They introduce Lynda Bogel, our professor. All of a sudden reality sets in. I am really going to do this? I am at Cornell and I am going to be part of a writing team. Most of the people in this class will probably be Cornell graduates and they will all have an interest in writing. After all, that is what they are here for. How intimidating.

I am back at the dorm and I am lying awake in my bed. There is a clock on the wall that says 1:30 a.m. The room is dark, but moonlight coming through the window illuminates the clock. I need to sleep in order to be sharp and rested for class. I close my eyes, but I cannot sleep. Each time I open my eyes the clock stares back at me, another hour gone.

By morning I am exhausted as the sunlight begins to peer through the window. The clock says 6:30 a.m. Class is at 9:00 a.m. I shower, get dressed, have a quick breakfast, and head for class.

I walk into the classroom and take a seat around a long conference table. There are thirteen of us in the class. Is this a lucky or unlucky number? Lynda Bogel, our teacher, is the last to arrive. She introduces herself and then asks us to go around the table and introduce ourselves, speak about our backgrounds, and what we are expecting to get out of the course.

As each person speaks about himself or herself, I am getting the sinking feeling that this is not a beginner's class at all. Most of the people in the class seem to know each other. Sara tells us she is a contributing writer for a Long Island newspaper: "I am so happy to be back at Cornell with all my old friends. I have been coming to this class for years."

Dede speaks next: "I am also so glad to be back at Cornell this year. My week-long course in Iowa last summer was wonderful, but I missed the group. I am an editor at Milward Brown, an educational materials company."

Elizabeth tells us she is a labor relations mediator and motivator for a private leadership program in Philadelphia. She is writing an important report and is looking for ideas.

Susan is Cornell's chaplain and has published two books on ethics.

Sue has come from California. She tells us she is a Cornell graduate with a degree in English and is writing her memoirs for her grandchildren.

Mary Kate is also a graduate and has been in the writing group for years.

They haven't gotten to me yet. I am ready to make a mad dash for the door. What have I gotten myself into? I was worried about having

Jackie, a friend from home who is an English teacher, in the class. She is a novice compared to these heavy hitters.

Charles is next. He tells us he is here because he has been asked by Cornell to write his memoirs for posterity. Who is Charles? I wonder. He is probably a famous novelist.

Then there is Harry. He seems the most senior in the group. He tells us he's here for kicks and to share war stories. It is his twenty-sixth year at the CAU writing class for beginners.

Only Bren seems to be in the same league as me. She lives in Ithaca and has an interest in nature and poetry.

Jackie introduces herself: "I am Jackie from Branchburg, New Jersey. I teach English at Raritan Valley Community College. I have a great interest in writing, and I am looking for inspiration to write on new subjects."

Last but least, it is my turn. I slowly rise as I feel my legs trembling and my voice quivering. Get a hold of yourself, I tell myself. "Hi, I am Evelyn Rauch from New Jersey. I am an interior designer and a mother of two children. Jackie and I are friends, as you might have guessed. I have no background in writing. I have a story I want to tell that I want my children to know. I have been trying to write it for years. I need guidance. I thought this was a beginner's course. I hope I didn't make a mistake."

Lynda Bogel quickly assures me that I am indeed in the right place and that I have nothing to worry about, which of course makes me terribly worried. I feel I have made a total fool of myself. What am I doing here? I must have been drunk when I decided to do this.

Professor Bogel gives an overview of what is expected of us for the week. "Tomorrow you will all bring a writing sample that you are prepared to read out loud in class. It can be on any subject—just a short piece so we can all have an idea of each other's writing style. Then we will critique each other. After that, we will all work on either a new piece or one that you wish to improve on. Each day several of you will read and the rest of us will comment. There will also be exercises meant to help stimulate discussion and new ideas. Have a nice afternoon, and see you tomorrow. I look forward to a great week."

It is Monday morning at 9:00 a.m. All thirteen of my new classmates are sitting around the conference table in our corner classroom. There is barely room to pass from seat to seat. No way to escape. Lynda welcomes us to our first day of class. Sara is the first one to read. Her piece is entitled "Life's Lessons and Lemonade." It is light and well written. She definitely has her own style and reads with confidence. I can tell she has done this many times before.

Next is Harry. Just a short poem from him, but he has us in stitches. I can tell if things get too heavy this week, Harry will be our comic relief.

Dede, another longtime member of this distinguished group agrees to read next. Her piece is so well written it is obvious that this is her vocation and she is no beginner. The story, about her dog, is entitled, "An Accidental Agility Addict."

Sue is writing a memoir for her grandchildren. She tells us she wants them to know what it was like growing up with parents who lived through the Great Depression and how money was always an issue in her home. The writing sample she has brought is beautifully written. It has such a tender touch. I can see these seasoned writers can write about anything and make it captivating and entertaining. Their subjects are ordinary, but their style of writing makes their stories come alive. Some of them have written all their lives. They come from varied backgrounds, but all have the same desire to communicate their thoughts and stories in the best way they know how.

So here I am. I, too, have that desire. I guess that is why I am sitting in this room with all these strangers. So, Evelyn, do you have the guts to get up and read? To humble yourself in front of your peers? I am shaking, but I know what I have to do. Slowly I stand up. I start to read, knowing that this is not going to move anyone. But I am here to learn and I have to start somewhere.

Lynda Bogel is the first one to comment. "Not a bad start. But you need to tell us why this is all so important. You need to have a hook, something to draw the reader in."

I answer, "I know, I just haven't found it yet. That is why I am here."

"Well think about what it is you're trying to tell us and then go for it. Don't skirt around it—just go for it." Sara says.

Mary Kate tells me that I need to grab the reader, but don't tell all right away or there will not be an element of surprise. They have no idea what I have been through.

I have taken the first step. I am here sitting in this room with people who know how to write down their thoughts in a skillful way. I can only hope that the energy generated in this room will rub off on me and propel me forward. It is so very scary to face myself in this way. Here with strangers, will I be able to bare my soul?

Lynda checks her watch. It is 12:30 p.m. "Well ladies and gentle-man, I think we have come to the end of this session. Each day we will break for lunch. From 2:00 p.m. to 5:00 p.m. I will have office hours and we will schedule individual conferences to go over your writing. You can work on your pieces and discuss them at these appointments. I will leave a list for you to sign up and I will pick it up after lunch." At this moment a young man enters the room. Lynda introduces him. "Ari will be our assistant for the week. You will send him your papers by e-mail each evening. Hopefully not at too late an hour and he will make enough copies for everyone for the next day's reading. If you have any computer problems, he is the man to see. You can use any of the campus computers or if you have your own computer that's fine, just make sure you get hooked up to the Cornell Ethernet. Okay, all you fellow scribblers go forth and have a productive day. Tomorrow we will continue reading. Please see me if you have any scheduling problems for our individual conferences."

I'm not sure whether to sign up for a conference today. What will I discuss? I am not happy with what I read in class, but I came here to learn how to write my mother's story and I do need help. So I sign up for a conference at 2:30 p.m.

At my meeting with Lynda I tell her that my mother and grandmother escaped from Nazi Germany and that I want my children and their children to know the story of their grandparents and great-grandparents before it is lost forever. I tell her that my mother died very suddenly and that it was a great shock to me, but I can't bring myself to tell her how she died. I'm not sure I need to. After all, this is going to be a story about my mother's and grandmother's life. As we continue to talk about their lives, Lynda senses that I am holding something back.

She asks, "Why have you decided to write this now? What has brought you to this decision at this moment in time?"

I look her straight in the eye and say, "My mother killed herself. That is why I have to do this. I have to leave something other than this horrible memory to my children. I want them to know that my mother and grandmother were survivors in every sense of the word. I want them to understand that life's deep disappointments brought my mother to this end and that for so long she had toughed life out. Her life had been a nightmare from beginning to end, but she had stayed strong for so long. I want them to know these people, to feel the blood that flowed in their veins, to understand their struggle, and to be proud of their grandmother rather than ashamed."

Lynda takes my hand. She has tears in her eyes. "Then tell the reader just what you told me. Find a symbol, something for the reader to hold onto. Keep it simple. Not too many words. Just tell us what you have been skirting around. Let us hear it. Be honest."

I can hardly hold back the tears. "I have been tiptoeing around the elephant in the room for years, afraid to confront my true motivation for writing this. How do I begin? I am scared to go forward; terrified to relive those terrible days when she died."

Lynda stands up. "You will find your voice," she says. She gives me an encouraging hug. "I'm afraid our conference has to end now, we've gone way over time and there is someone waiting to go next. I'm looking forward to hearing your mother's story. Remember, keep it simple and find a hook to draw the reader in. Just take it "bird by bird." See you tomorrow."

The tension in my body is unbearable. I am so conflicted and hoping that somehow, someway the inspiration to write this story will come to me. That by some divine intervention I will be enlightened.

My room at Ecology House is very sparse. There are two beds and two desks with two chairs. The walls are painted medium beige and there are no paintings on the walls and no window treatments, just a set of blinds that are bent and broken in several places. There are two lamps with sixty-watt bulbs. At night the light is dim. The only embellishment on the wall is a clock, which ticks loudly and has kept me up the last two nights. It reminds me of the clock on the wall in my mother's hospital room; the monotonous sound of each minute ticking away slowly, but continuously. I sit at one of the desks with my laptop open. I try to start again on Steffi's story. It is 9:00 p.m. I feel a sense of emptiness. I can't bring myself to put on paper what it is I want to say. Each attempt is worse than the next. I hit the delete key on the computer and try again.

I look up again at the clock on the wall. It's 12:30 a.m. I think I will never be able to tell this story. I'm tired, tired of all of this; tired of trying. I should go to bed and get some rest. Why am I doing this anyway? My children have moved on. Why can't I? Why is this so important to me? As I look at the barren landscape around this room I realize that the reason this is so important is because the connection to family, the thread that weaves us all together is the only thing that really matters. That is why I am here. That is why I have to find a way to express the inexpressible.

My mind is searching for the answer to how to move forward. Moving forward. That's it. I realize this is a timeline. The clock, the clock on the wall, it's the only thing that is moving in this room, and it was the only thing moving in the room that my mother occupied in the hospital. That's it. That's my hook. That is how this story is going to come together. Lynda said to keep it simple, use a hook to grab the reader, and just tell the story. The clock has been ticking away the seconds, minutes, hours, months, and years of our lives. It's so simple. It has been staring me in the face all along.

I continue to write. The words are flying onto the page. My emotions are uncontainable. I can hardly write between the tears. All that I have been holding inside for so long is bursting out of me. My heart is so full. Pain, love, anger, and excitement are flooding my body. I am being swept away in a sea of emotion. My heart is pounding in my chest. I can hardly contain myself as I sit at the computer and go on. I type without stopping to catch my breath; each line flows into the next like a river going downstream to the sea. I can't stop. The momentum of my story is now pulling me along and I am caught up in the moment. I have been captured and sent back in time to those terrible days in January of 1999, back to my mother's hospital room. I am reliving those horrible days leading up to my mother's death. The only sound in my room is that of the clock ticking away the seconds as each strike on the keyboard brings forth another flow of feelings. Hours have passed by like seconds. My computer screen reveals the first draft of what I suppose will be the beginning of my story.

For Lynda Bogel, my mentor:

It is the last day of class and Lynda hands me a small paperback. The title brings a smile: *Bird by Bird: Some Instructions on Writing and Life* by Anne Lamott. Inside is a small inscription:

Evelyn,
How do you write your mother and you?
Bird by bird.
Keep sharing with me as your writing
---And life----go on!
Lynda

Mother Keeper of my Soul

I shunned you when I should have embraced you.
You were so hard on me, so filled with expectations never met.
Your love too intense to be returned.
Now I long for your deep unwavering love.
I long for your tender touch;
Your comforting arms.
I need your guidance.
How lonely it is without a mother.
How empty I feel without your love.
How hollow the caverns of my mind.
How deep the sting in my heart.
Mother, I love you so!